THE CLOUDS SHOULD KNOW ME BY NOW

For Philip Whalen

THE CLOUDS
SHOULD KNOW ME
BY NOW

Buddhist
Poet
Monks
of
China

Edited by
RED PINE &
MIKE O'CONNOR

Introduction by
ANDREW SCHELLING

Translations by
PAUL HANSEN
MIKE O'CONNOR
RED PINE
JAMES SANFORD
J.P. SEATON
BURTON WATSON

Wisdom

Wisdom Publications
199 Elm Street
Somerville, MA 02144
wisdompubs.org

Library of Congress Cataloging-in-Publication Data
The clouds should know me by now : Buddhist poet monks of China /
    edited by Red Pine & Mike O'Connor ; introduction by Andrew
    Schelling ; translations by Paul Hansen ... [et al.].
        p.   cm.
    Includes bibliographical references and index.
    ISBN 0-86171-143-2 (alk. paper)
        1. Chinese poetry—Buddhist authors—Translations into English.
    I. Pine, Red. II. O'Connor, Mike.
    PL2658.E3C65   1998
    895.1'0080922943—DC21   98-17768

ISBN 978-0-86171-143-7   ebook ISBN 978-0-86171-953-2

19 18 17 16
8   7   6   5

Cover and interior design by: Gopa&Ted2, Inc. Set in Bembo 10.5/14 pt.
Chinese Typesetting by: Birdtrack Press, New Haven, Connecticut
Cover image: Huangshan, China. Photo by: Steven R. Johnson

Contents

Clambering up the Cold Mountain path,
The Cold Mountain trail goes on and on:
The long gorge choked with scree and boulders,
The wide creek, the mist-blurred grass.
The moss is slippery, though there's been no rain.
The pine sings, but there's no wind.
Who can leap the world's ties
And sit with me among the white clouds?

—*Han-shan*
(Translation by Gary Snyder)

PREFACE

CHINA'S CONFUCIAN ELITE weren't the only ones who wrote poems. Buddhist monks also practiced the art that combined insight with the emptiness of language and the harmonies of the human voice. When the Fifth Patriarch wanted to appoint a successor, he asked for a poem. And the poem he accepted as worthy of the robe and bowl of Bodhidharma was from an illiterate kitchen worker. For many Buddhists the ability to compose a poem was just as important as a knowledge of ritual or scripture. For some it was more so. The poem was the lion's roar and the hermit's sigh.

But while China's monks have often been as prolific as scholar-officials in the writing of verse, little of their work has been translated into Western languages—the poems of Han-shan (Cold Mountain) being the rare exception. The purpose of this book, then, is to introduce several more voices of this Buddhist poetic lineage. To this end, each of the translators has chosen the work of a poet monk (or a group of them in Paul Hansen's case) largely unknown in the West.

Before passing on the results of our joint efforts to the reader, the editors would like to thank those without whose collaboration this book would not have been published. First, we would like to acknowledge the impetus given to this project by Albert A. Dalia, former editorial director of Wisdom Publications. The editors have talked about many books that disappeared with the sunset. Albert kept this one in the sky, as did the publisher, Tim McNeill. Moreover, both encouraged our active participation in the book's design, accommodating, for example, our desire to include the Chinese text. Nothing gives us greater pleasure than to put such a useful and finely made book in the hands of readers. For this opportunity, we are most grateful.

We are also grateful to our fellow translators. It would have been hard to assemble a more accomplished group. Not only are all long-time students of Buddhist practice and Chinese literature, they are also able poets and have taken the time to search beyond the words for the spirit of the poems they have translated.

Thanks too to J.P. Seaton for including a selection of these translations in the Summer 1998 issue of *The Literary Review*.

We also thank Andrew Schelling for providing readers a match with which to burn these incense lines and Steve Johnson for contributing his cover photograph of Huangshan that evokes their setting. Finally, we thank Gary Snyder for the opening Han-shan translation and Finn Wilcox for the book's closing poem recalling a journey to the sacred mountain of Chiuhuashan and his encounter with a lone Buddhist nun whose closest neighbors were tigers. Thus does the present form a bridge to the past.

The Editors
Port Townsend, Washington
Spring, Year of the Tiger

EDITORS' NOTE: In romanizing Chinese names and words, the translators have used variations of the Wade-Giles system, though an occasional inconsistency may sometimes appear. Some geographical locations, for instance, have been rendered in Pinyin style to reflect the way they are spelled on contemporary maps of China. Also, both *Zen* and *Ch'an* are used to refer to the transmission of understanding begun in China by Bodhidharma. *Ch'an* is the Wade-Giles romanization of the modern Mandarin pronunciation, while *Zen* represents the standard romanization of the Japanese pronunciation, by means of which the world has learned of this tradition.

INTRODUCTION
Andrew Schelling

GNARLED PINES, wind-blown clouds, jutting mountain pinnacles, exiled scholars, horses, trailing willows. Moonlight on meandering rivers, fishermen, white cranes and mandarin ducks, the eerie screech of a gibbon, tiny white plum blossoms on twisted branches, a battered wooden boat moored in the distance. For more than a thousand years the poets in this book wandered a landscape that is vast and at the same time intimate, mysterious, and deeply familiar: the same mountain peaks, the same villages, the same river gorges. What makes this landscape feel so much like home? The old poets of China had a way of quickly getting down to elemental things. Using a vocabulary of tangible, ordinary objects, they composed unsentimental poems that seem the precise size of a modest human life—the reflective sadness, the fleeting calm pleasures.

This book is a collection of poetry written by Ch'an Buddhist poet monks *(shih-seng)*, men of enviable literary talent who lived out their years during turbulent times in accord with old Buddha's precepts. Their work spans 1100 years, from the middle T'ang dynasty to the beginning of the twentieth century. One or two have had a taste of renown in the West, on the basis of a couple of poems, but the rest have gone unheralded. Several were established Buddhist teachers of their own day, the influence of their subtle minds reaching deep, but they had little reputation as poets. Recognition of their literary efforts comes late. Only Chia Tao, the earliest of the poets translated here, did not devote his adult life to Buddhist monasticism. He slipped off the monk's "robe of patches" in his early thirties to pursue a life of poetry, which he supported with marginal government employment and years of inadequate pay. One lingers over the detail: at the time of his death, his only worldly possessions were a five-string zither and an ailing donkey. Chia Tao stuck by his decision to make poetry a life's path, but a hint of regret sometimes lifts from his verse.

As Buddhists, these men traveled a great deal. When reading their poems you observe how deliberately they led, as Thoreau would have put it, hyper-ethereal lives—"under the open sky." It is no accident, then, that a prevalent theme in the poetry is the farewell poem for a comrade, typically situated at daybreak after a night of wine or tea, vivid talk, or silent companionship. These poets spent their days living in and journeying between the numerous Buddhist sites of pre-modern China—village temples, remote points of pilgrimage, monasteries tucked deep within forests, the mountain yogin's hut in a secluded mossy gulch. The politics of those eleven centuries were shifty and uncertain as well. Scholars, poets, civil servants, Buddhist abbots, and even monks of no reputation were driven from region to region, into exile through wind-blown mountain passes, or when the regime shifted, recalled up a thundering river gorge to serve in some official capacity.

Mountains, forests, and rivers make up the well-known landscapes of Chinese painting. In the poetry a clipped, selective vocabulary, surprisingly ambiguous in the Chinese originals, merely suggests "what's out there." It is up to the reader to fill in the details — tumbling watercourses, looming peaks, twisted mountain strata, low-land pools, deer and wild gibbons, wind-stunted trees. Always alongside the poet, nonhuman creatures move easily in the world of his poem. Deer and wild cranes follow their own tracks, but their travels seem to meaningfully crisscross the poet's. At times untamed creatures become, with only a touch of irony, profound teachers for the wandering-cloud poets. And by an interesting karmic twist, these various citizens of Chinese verse have in recent decades sensitized American readers to distinct features of our own continent: watersheds, seasonal cycles, animal habits, plant successions, and the like.

Not surprisingly, three of the six translators of the present collection have made their homes in the Pacific Northwest, where the natural world—dark clutching forests, shy owls, concealing mists, abrupt icy pinnacles lit by a fugitive ray of sun—so resembles the setting of a Chinese poem. Across the centuries you can hear Chia Tao asking, "Where is the master? Gathering herbs, off on the mountain, hidden by clouds."

Beyond a presentation of poems about the natural world, this collection offers possible examples of what in Chinese has been called *shih-shu*, "rock-and-bark poetry." In 1703 one of the poets translated here assumed this term for a *nom de plume*, and craftily hid his identity behind it. It is uncertain how widely the phrase circulated, but *shih-shu* were colloquially written, mildly irreverent poems, not simply skeptical of city-folk hustle or merely celebratory of reclusive hours spent in savage wilderness settings. Rather than being brushed on silk or paper, *shih-shu* were written on scraps of bamboo, scratched into bark, on rocks, or pecked into cliff faces. The notorious practitioner of this genre, and maybe the originator of *shih-shu*, is the poet Han-shan (possibly seventh century), who is known to American readers as Cold Mountain. Translations by R.H. Blyth, Gary Snyder, Red Pine, and Burton Watson have made Han-shan well known in recent decades.

According to Lu-ch'iu Yin, a minor T'ang government official and Buddhist enthusiast, Han-shan's *gatha*, or Buddhist verse, were left littered about the forbidding cliff from which he took his name. The Han-shan promontory lies along the T'ien-t'ai range in Chekiang, a strikingly wild country in southern China. Contemporary photographs show cornfields beneath the rock wall, but in Han-shan's day it was heavily forested land, and local woodcutters or monks occasionally saw the poet disappear into a cave, which in some unsettling accounts would close up behind him.

Unable to coax Han-shan into establishing closer ties to the world of civilized people (Han-shan just giggled, threw things, and ran into the woods) the well-intended Lu-ch'iu Yin sent a troop of men into the mountains to collect what of the scattered poems they could find—about three hundred in total. The legend of ragged Han-shan and his equally eccentric comrade Shih-te became a reference for countless later poets, who saw in their cryptic behavior—as much as in their poetry—a deep Buddhist realization. In the 1960s, California poet Lew Welch, much taken with Chinese scholar poems and the habits of Ch'an hermits, is said to have left the sole copy of one of his poems tacked to a barroom wall in Sausalito.

The karma runs deep. In the late 1980s a group of American poets gathered one spring at Green Gulch Farm's Zen Center, twenty minutes north of Sausalito, to talk about poetry and Buddhist meditation. It marked the first time such an event had been convened east of the Bering Strait. Open to the public, the gathering hosted the usual cast of characters: blue-jeans bodhisattvas, long-haired yogins, quick-witted yoginis, nautch girls, coyote men, patch-robe monastics, and unemployed scholars. The gathering caught the echo of earlier events, "Ch'an guests and poetry masters," that by the eighth century had become regular practice in China.

That weekend, in a pond in back of the drafty Green Gulch zendo, a frog sangha held its own convocation—like the gibbons and wild cranes of Chinese verse? Many good remarks were made during the conferences, but one in particular has stuck with me. The poet-priest Norman Fischer, in a very unsensational fashion, said, "Meditation is when you sit down and do nothing. Poetry is when you sit down and do something." With these sage words, he neatly wiped out centuries of debate—in India, China, and Japan—over whether poetry is a legitimate pursuit for the earnest Buddhist in search of realization.

Yes, meditation and poetry. It is hard to imagine with what sobriety the early Buddhists in India enjoined monks and nuns against literary pursuits. It is equally striking that as late as 817 c.e. the renowned Po Chu-i could write:

Since earnestly studying the Buddhist doctrine of emptiness,
I've learned to still all the common states of mind.

Only the devil of poetry I have yet to conquer—
let me come on a bit of scenery and I start my idle droning.

(translation by Burton Watson)

Without doubt, these two distinctly human undertakings, making songs and watching the mind, go inestimably far back into prehistory. Would our contemporary North American consumer culture offer a bemused smile to the notion of a conflict between them? Aspirants watch out! Remember Chia Tao's zither and old sick donkey! There seems so little time these days, and hopelessly little reward, for practicing either. Yet a not-so-secret, and surprisingly durable, counterculture keeps the two alive, evidently unable to do without either. Often the two get pursued hand in hand, or, as Norman Fischer noted, in nearly the same posture. Luckily, as North Americans, we don't have to cut back too much growth in order to keep the hall of practice clear. Behind us stand heartening documents from Asia, compiled over the course of several thousand years, to show what others have done.

Over the last few centuries, the poetry movements from Europe, England, and America—such as Romanticism, Symbolism, Pre-Raphaelitism, Futurism, Vorticism, Dada, Surrealism, Mythopoetics, Fluxus, and Language Poetry—have made powerful breaks with the past. Poets need to confront our disordered human realm, its conflicts and anguish, and the work has been heroically done. Yet there's relief when the poems of old China, steeped in Buddhist or Taoist thought, come forward to point another path through the modern world. Influenced by Buddhist and Taoist views of nature, Chinese poetry *(shih)* has helped invigorate an American poetry that's willing to wander away from bustling human settlements. Yet the social impasses and agonies, the stuff of being all-too-human, don't disappear; they simply move for a moment into the moonlight when the Ch'an masters speak. And a landscape suffused with Buddhist emptiness comes forth.

Poems of friendship, family life, travel; poems with a breath of pine wind. They strike a tone that's seasoned, deeply and resolutely secular. Honesty, hard luck, good humor, close friends, a taste for simple things, tea, wine, moonlight. From the point of view of Buddhist doctrine, these poems are "invisible." Philosophical meaning lies hidden in the landscape, behind the trees, out in the mist. Dogma or preachiness would make the poem impudent.

Wang Wei (701–761), a Buddhist practitioner and a careful student of landscapes, established a further quality of much Ch'an poetry: the exclusion of anything grand, sensational, strenuous, or heroic. This is a very particular yogic restraint for the poem, and the discipline leaves us with men (and a few women) that sound like they could be talking to us directly. Certainly they know disorder, war, cruelty, and injustice—their grief is evident. But it's as though they attempt to rectify all that with a poetry that places little solitary humans in cloud-covered mountains.

Americans of many backgrounds, who not long ago admired and cultivated a lean, resolute character, were hungry for access to these traditions—the bitter tea of Ch'an Buddhism, a poetry with the taste of gnarled wood. After all, how many among us first learned poetry skills by rewriting some old Chinese poem? How many among us got a first taste of Zen by copying a detail out of the life of some Chinese hermit met in a book? Or saw an ink-brush scroll in which a thin stream drops from cloud-piercing pinnacles—then noticed a tiny pavilion, one quiet scholar gazing into the void—all done in a few confidant strokes?

It was only in 1915 that Chinese poetry first reached Western readers of poetry. Working from handwritten notebooks of maverick art historian Ernest Fenollosa, Ezra Pound put together a group of seventeen Chinese poems and called it *Cathay*. Although the title of the book recalls an era of British gunships and trade companies—"Cathay and the Way Thither"—the collection of poems, mostly translations from T'ang poet Li Po's work, points forward to a future that would know Asia, not as an overseas continent to be plundered for spice and fiber, but as a homeland to writers of a poetry that reads like a product of our own time. Pound published his book in London, midway through World War I. Many of his close comrades were holding the trenches in France—Henri Gaudier-Brzeska, Wyndham Lewis, Richard Aldington, and Ernest Hemingway—and some would be dead, others wounded, before the war was over. It is no surprise, then, that his attention went to poems about war's human cost: boyish conscripts holding outposts against a formidable enemy, lonely girls who should have had lovers, honest scholars brushed into exile. His book still stands as one of the best. But there was more to Chinese poetry.

Much of it came into translation after the Second World War. Scholars and soldiers who saw action in the Pacific theater brought back with them a bit of Asian culture. Kyoto in the mid-fifties developed a lively expatriate group of poets, translators, Zen students, and scholars. Young writers in the States, spurred to the modern flavor of *shih*, were able to book cheap passage to Asia by boat, or they journeyed there figuratively by staying home, drinking tea, and getting Chinese ideograms under their belts. One of the influential publications of the time was Gary Snyder's translation of twenty-four Han-shan poems (1958), which thousands of Americans read. That same year Jack Kerouac's book *The Dharma Bums* gave Han-shan and Zen Buddhism the flavor of cultural revolution. "I see a vision of a great rucksack revolution, thousands or even millions of young Americans wandering around with their rucksacks, going up the mountains to pray, making children laugh and old men glad...Zen lunatics who go about writing poems." Ch'an Buddhist poets seemed right up to date.

What was so modern about these old poets? Kenneth Rexroth wrote of Tu Fu (712–770): "Tu Fu comes from a saner, older, more secular culture than Homer, and it is not a new discovery with him that the gods, the abstractions and forces of nature, are frivolous, lewd, vicious, quarrelsome, and cruel, and only men's steadfastness, love, magnanimity, calmness, and compassion redeem the night-bound world." He also said, "Tu Fu is not religious at all. But for me his response to the human situation is the only kind of religion likely to outlast this century. 'Reverence for life,' it has been called."

Reverence for life (Sanskrit *ahimsa*: non-injury, no wanton killing) was a cornerstone of Buddhist practice in India long before a few first sutra literatures took the rugged northeast road into China, influencing Chia Tao and his poetry cohorts. Maybe we're in a position now to see that this is what's so compelling in 1500 years of Ch'an poetry. The best poems push no doctrine or dogma, there's no jingo, no proselytizing. The Buddhism is carefully hidden away in tight five- and seven-syllable lines. (This metric pattern, according to Yunte Huang, "is intimately related to the translations from the Sanskrit Buddhist texts. It was the encounter with an alphabetical language—Sanskrit—that made the Chinese realize for the first time that a Chinese character was pronounced by a combination of vowel and consonant.") There it lurks—archaic and instantly modern—a reverence for life: one's own, one's companions, one's fellow earth-dwelling creatures.

Ezra Pound compiled a book of Li Po's verse while young men across Europe were fighting in trenches. It seems he conceived *Cathay* as an anti-war book, not as propaganda, but as the effort a poet might make in order to shift the way people see things. Why is it that behind the stolid, often melancholy tone of so much Chinese verse—a tone long ago admiringly called "bland, like the taste of withered wood"—modern ears detect an acute comradeship with all forms of life? Nearly as far back as Chinese literature goes arises the term *the ten thousand things*, Taoist shorthand for the planet's numberless creatures. "Sentient beings are numberless, I vow to save them," goes the chant in the zendo. This camaraderie, or instant sense of warm-heartedness, is what makes such a contribution to Buddhist literature, to ecology ethics, and to postmodern poetry.

Chia Tao—	The solitary bird
loves the wood;
your heart also
not of the world.

| Ch'i-chi— | On my pillow bit by bit waking, suddenly I hear a single cicada cry — at that moment I know I have not died. |

Ch'i-chi—

On my pillow bit by bit waking,
suddenly I hear a single cicada cry —
at that moment I know I have not died.

Pao T'an—

Frosty wind
Raises deep night,
Missing only
A gibbon's howl.

Han-shan Te-ch'ing—

Who can be a wild deer among
        deserted mountains
satisfied with tall grass and pines

Shih-shu—

my heart is free as the white clouds
body light as a crimson leaf
apes and birds pull me forward

Ching An—

White clouds too know the flavor
of this mountain life

Dogen Zenji, the thirteenth-century Japanese philosopher versed in Ch'an practice, picked up the spirit in his own cranky, mischievous way—

That the self advances and confirms the ten thousand things
        is called delusion;
That the ten thousand things advance and confirm the self
        is called enlightenment.

There is good testimony that long familiarity with meditation—months, years, decades—contributes to a person's clear-headedness, focus, and good humor. Beyond such personal benefits, it's also possible you become a better citizen. A heightened sense of empathy seems to emerge—one that even crosses the boundaries between nature's "kingdoms," human, animal, insect, or plant. Tibetan Buddhists vow to liberate all beings, down to "the last blade of grass."

Perhaps there was a time when poetry didn't pay much attention to these things. But if the ecologists are right, we currently dwell in an epoch the future will know as "the great dying." Edward O. Wilson and other scientists give compelling evidence that we little humans are bringing about the fastest wave of species extinction known in the four-billion-year history of our blue-green planet. Maybe one of the consciousness-shifting tools we humans can use if we hope to turn this around is the poetry left by departed Chinese masters. I expect it will be the poems of invisible Buddhist insight, wrapped in mist or moonlight, and not the poems of an expressly dogmatic or doctrinal character, that will give us the best bearing.

So take a walk with the Ch'an buddha-ancestors, these cranky, melancholy, lonely, mischievous poet-ancestors. Their songs are stout as a pilgrim's stave or a pair of good shoes and were meant to be taken on the great journey. Even Han-shan Te-ch'ing—who ruined his legs from prolonged zazen and needed someone to carry him to his teapot, his writing table, his gate, or his window—even he wrote poetry that flies with the cranes, crisscrosses slopes with the deer, drifts with the white clouds. If it all seems ordinary to you, well, it should. Whoever said poetry or Buddhism was anything unusual?

Boulder, Colorado

賈島

Chia Tao (779–843)

Translations by Mike O'Connor

Introduction

CHIA TAO WAS A BUDDHIST POET of the Middle T'ang dynasty. Born into an impoverished family near today's Beijing, he became a Ch'an (Zen) monk early in his youth, with the religious name Wu-pen. While scant biographical detail of his monastic days exists, his official biography does note that upon arriving at the Eastern Capital, Lo-yang, Chia Tao wrote a poem protesting a curfew forbidding monks to go out after noon. The poem caught the sympathetic eye of the eminent Confucian poet Han Yu (768–824) and led to the latter becoming Chia Tao's poetry mentor.

A more famous account—a literary anecdote—describes the meeting of the poets this way: Chia Tao, while riding a donkey on the way to the marketplace, was deeply absorbed in trying to choose between two words, push (*t'ui*) and knock (*ch'iao*) in the line "Under the moon, a monk [knocks at, or pushes] the gate." Reciting the line over and over, Chia Tao became oblivious of his surroundings and collided with a sedan chair carrying Han Yu. Han Yu, waving off apologies from Chia Tao, became interested in his poetic impasse, and immediately opted for the word "knock." The compound "push-knock (*t'ui-ch'iao*)" thereafter became the traditional term to describe, not only Chia Tao's assiduousness of craft, but any poet's exacting labor to find the *mot juste,* or to make careful stylistic distinctions.

What is known factually is that Chia Tao, at about age thirty-one, abandoned monasticism to devote himself to a secular life of poetry, supported by subsistence civil service. He was encouraged in this by a circle of prominent poets, including Han Yu, Meng

Chiao (751–814) and Chang Chi (ca. 776–ca. 829). The group was based in the political and literary capital Ch'ang-an, modern Xi'an, the largest city in the world at the time and Chia Tao's principal home until his "banishment" late in life to provincial posts—an apparent victim of slander.

Although he left the Buddhist order, his heart never really left the world of "mountains and clouds"—the secluded communities of religious adepts who were dedicated to some form of the Way (Tao), and whose practices collectively brought forth one of the great religious ages. Though his poems reveal that he chided himself for not being more deeply realized, it may be that his sense of limitation in this regard only enhanced his admiration of those who were.

As a poet with a monk's background, he was welcome at temples and hermitages alike. He was, in fact, given the literary name Lang-hsien, Wandering Immortal, and his poems record his sojourns among not only the religious elements—clerics, poet monks, and hermits—but among the lay community of literati as well.

If Chia Tao's search for Buddhist enlightenment was an unfulfilled one, so too was his search for a significant civil-service position. In fact, it is not clear that he ever passed the examination and received his *chin-shih* degree. In his mature years, his deepest quest was for poetic mastery and, related to this, in finding *chih-yin*, people who understood and appreciated his poetry—a time-honored quest in Chinese literary history.

Chia Tao writes a quietistic poem that features nothing more dramatic than a parting, a viewing of landscape, thoughts of a distant friend, or a stay overnight. Atmosphere, or mood, in many instances, is what the poem is most about. His lyrical work at its purest has the beauty of inhospitable, or remote, mountains; yet when speaking to themes of friendship, Chia Tao's human empathy is the measure of the peaks. The edge of sorrow running through his poems was honed in part by his chronic poverty, but it rarely gives way to bitterness or self-pity.

Though the poet does not overtly preach the Dharma, his life

and training as a monk naturally influenced his artistic tempera-
ment: the poems are spare, technically hard-won (*t'ui-ch'iao*), and
morally serious. In his early discursive poems, probably influenced
by Han Yu, Confucian values surface as well.

As with the poet monks, Chia Tao's poems are filled with the
imagery of remote temples and stone chimes, looming peaks and
wind-twisted pines. But with Chia Tao, as with Wang Wei (701–
761) before him, Buddhism is largely internalized; its expression is
aesthetic, not philosophical.

Some of Chia Tao's contemporaries and literary descendants
found his poems inclined to pessimism, and the poet Su Tung-p'o
(1037–1101) wrote critically that Chia Tao's work was "lean" and
Meng Chiao's "cold." Meng Chiao, upon first encountering the
tall, imposing figure of the younger Chia Tao, even called him "a
lean monk lying in ice"—and this from an old poet who himself
was a poverty-saddled recluse!

Chia Tao's extant poems number four hundred and four. Of
these, the "Farewell Poem" is most widely represented, accounting
for nearly one hundred. As scholars have pointed out, this poetic
subcategory resonated deeply with Chinese of the T'ang era, owing
to the huge distances of China, the rudimentary transportation,
and the strong ties of friendship and family. For Chia Tao, a poem
on the theme of farewell was, at least ritualistically, a gift to the
traveler, as well as a means for the poet to ease his own sadness of
separation.

His favored poetic form was the *lu-shih*, or the regulated form
of the eight-line verse. In this form each line contains either five
or seven characters, obeys rules for rhyme, and has verbal and tonal
parallelisms. Tu Fu's (712–770) achievement in this form was a standard for poets such as Chia Tao, who came on the scene after the
High T'ang period. Chia Tao refined the form and took certain
liberties with it, thereby gaining many disciples in the Late T'ang
and beyond.

The poet died in humble circumstances. His only known
possessions were an ailing donkey and a five-string zither. He was

survived by his wife, but no children. Still, Chia Tao never anticipated worldly rewards. He attained a high degree of poetic excellence that has earned his poetry grateful readers down to the present. And in the course of his arduous life, he had the consolation of enjoying the friendship of the leading scholars, poets, and sages of his time. As Chia Tao put it, writing on the occasion of a visit from his friend Yung T'ao:

> Not having to be alone
> is happiness;
> we do not talk
> of failure or success.

冬夜送人

平明走馬上村橋花落梅溪雪未消
日短天寒愁送客楚山無限路迢迢

WINTER NIGHT FAREWELL

At first light, you ride
swiftly over the village bridge;

Plum blossoms fall
on the stream and unmelted snow.

With the days short and the weather cold,
it's sad to see a guest depart;

The Ch'u Mountains are boundless,
and the road, remote.

MEMENTO ON THE DEPARTURE
OF A FRIEND FROM YEH,
LAST DAY OF THE SECOND MOON

In flowering willows,
we rein in our horses;
at parting, we are free
to drink all the wine we desire.

But the winds of spring
sweep slowly north;
clouds and wild geese
do not fly south.

Tomorrow
dawns the first—
already the third
month of the year!

Touch whip to lean horse and go
into the colors of dusk;
mist is rising
on far peaks.

二月晦日留別鄂中友人
立馬柳花裏別君當酒酣春風漸向北雲鴈不飛南
明曉日初一今年月又三鞭羸去暮色遠岳起煙嵐

早行

早起赴前程鄰雞尚未鳴主人燈下別羸馬暗中行
蹋石新霜滑穿林宿鳥驚遠山鐘動後曙色漸分明

MORNING TRAVEL

Rising early
to begin the journey;
not a sound
from the chickens next door.

Beneath the lamp,
I part from the innkeeper;
on the road, my skinny horse
moves through the dark.

Slipping on stones
newly frosted,
threading through woods,
we scare up birds roosting.

After a bell tolls
far in the mountains,
the colors of daybreak
gradually clear.

PASSING BY A MOUNTAIN VILLAGE AT DUSK

For several *li*,
I've been hearing the cold stream;
mountain villagers
have few near neighbors.

Strange birds
cry in the wild;
the setting sun
gives pause to the traveler.

A new moon shines,
but won't last the night;
border signal towers
do not reach past Ch'in.

Beyond the scraggly
mulberry grove—
cook smoke
coming closer.

暮過山村
數里聞寒水山家少
四鄰怪禽啼曠野落日恐行人
初月未終夕邊烽不過秦蕭條桑柘外煙火漸相親

宿山寺

眾岫聳寒色精廬向此分星透疏木走月逆行雲

絕頂人來少高松鶴不群一僧年八十世事未曾聞

OVERNIGHT AT A BUDDHIST
MOUNTAIN TEMPLE

Massed peaks pierce
the cold-colored sky;
a view
the monastery faces.

Shooting stars pass
into sparse-branched trees;
the moon travels one way,
clouds the other.

Few people come
to this mountaintop;
cranes do not flock
in the tall pines.

One Buddhist monk,
eighty years old,
has never heard
of the world's affairs.

FAREWELL TO MONK CHIH-HSING

You have lived a long time
at Pa-hsing Temple;
retired, you're preparing
only now to leave.

On the verge of parting, we look
out upon the bright water of autumn;
you're not returning to your hometown
nor to the countryside near it.

You will hang your Buddhist staff in a tree
where the sky reaches to a watery horizon;
where the door-leaf of your hut
opens on great mountains.

Below, you will see dawn
a thousand *li* away:
a miniature sun
born of a cold white sea.

錫久送
掛住知
天巴興
涯興上
樹寺人
房如
開今
嶽始
頂拂
扉衣
下欲
看臨
萬秋
里水
曉別
霜不
海向
日故
生園
微歸

雪晴晚望

倚杖望晴雪溪雲幾萬重樵人歸白屋寒日下危峰

野火燒岡草斷煙生石松卻迴山寺路聞打暮天鐘

WATCHING THE LATE DAY CLEAR
AFTER SNOWFALL

Leaning on my staff,
I watch the sky clearing after snow;
clouds are layered high
over the mountain stream.

As the woodcutter
returns to his hut,
a cold sun sets
on perilous peaks.

A farmer's fire
burns the grass along a ridge;
wisps of cook smoke rise
in rock-girt pines.

Returning to the temple
along the mountain road,
I hear the striking
of the evening bell.

AT I-CHOU, CLIMBING THE TOWER
OF LUNG-HSING TEMPLE
TO VIEW THE HIGH NORTHERN MOUNTAINS

The tallest peaks
north of the district—
cliffs so high
they block cloud paths.

At dawn,
I climb the tower for a look,
gradually feeling
their serene effect.

In smoke-blue
haze,
massed peaks
appear as if joined.

When will I climb
and set foot there,
to gaze on all
creation below?

朦　郡　易
朧　北　州
碧　最　登
煙　高　龍
裏　峰　興
群　巉　寺
嶺　巖　樓
若　絕　望
相　雲　郡
附　路　北
何　朝　高
時　來　峰
一　上
登　樓
陟　望
萬　稍
物　覺
皆　幽
下　趣
顧

尋隱者不遇

松下問童子言師採藥去只在此山中雲深不知處

SEEKING BUT NOT FINDING THE RECLUSE

Under pines
I ask the boy;

he says: "My Master's gone
to gather herbs.

I only know
he's on this mountain,

but the clouds are too deep
to know where."

WRITTEN AT THE DWELLING OF A RECLUSE

Even though you have a brushwood door,
it hasn't been shut for a long time;

A few clouds, a few trees
have been your only companions.

Still, I suspect if you stay longer,
people will learn of this spot;

We'll see you moving
higher on the mountain.

題隱者居
雖有柴門長不關片雲孤木伴身閑猶嫌住久人知處
見擬移家更上山

草合徑微微　終南對掩扉　晚涼疏雨絕　初曉遠蟬稀
落葉無青地　閒身著白衣　朴愚猶本性　不是學忘機
茺齋

ABODE OF THE UNPLANNED EFFECT

The grass–covered path
is secluded and still;
a closed door faces
the Chungnan Mountains.

In the evening, the air's chilly,
but the light rain stops;
at dawn, far off,
a few cicadas start.

Leaves fall
where no green earth remains;
a person at his ease,
wears a plain, white robe.

With simplicity and plainness
his original nature still,
what need to practice
"calming of the heart?"

A FAREWELL TO T'IEN CHO
ON RETREAT ON HUA MOUNTAIN

Deep and hidden, cicadas
fill the dusk;
startled, you awaken
from a stone-bed sleep.

Near your hut,
a waterfall
falls
thousands of feet.

Pines near the altar
drip dew;
the mountain moon
shines in vast, clear space.

When a crane passes over,
you must see—
riderless, it should bear
an immortal.

送田卓入華山
幽深足暮蟬驚覺石床眠瀑布五千仞草堂瀑布邊
壇松涓滴露嶽月沈寥天鶴過君須看上頭應有仙

孟融逸人

孟君臨水居不食水中魚
衣褐唯麤帛筐箱祇素書
樹林幽鳥戀世界此心疏
擬棹孤舟去何峰又結廬

MENG JUNG, GAINFULLY UNEMPLOYED

Your residence, Meng,
overlooks the river;
but you do not eat
the fish in it.

Your robe is common,
sewn of coarse cloth;
silk books alone
fill your bamboo shelves.

The solitary bird
loves the wood;
your heart also
not of the world.

You plan to row away
in a lone boat, and
build another hut—
in which mountains?

WHILE TRAVELING

With so much on my mind,
it's hard to express myself in letters.

How long has it been since I left home?
Old friends are no longer young.

Frosted leaves fall into empty bird nests;
river fireflies weave through open windows.

I stop at a forest monk's,
and spend the night in "quiet sitting."

旅遊

此心非一事書札若爲傳舊國別多日故人無少年
空巢霜葉落疏牖水螢穿留得林僧宿中宵坐默然

送褚山人歸日東
懸帆待秋水去入杳冥關東海幾年別中華此日還
岸遙生白髮波盡露青山隔水相思在無書也是閑

SEEING OFF THE MOUNTAIN MONK CH'U,
RETURNING TO JAPAN

Sail spread, you're ready
to depart on autumn waters,
to enter a deep, far realm
between realms.

Away from the Eastern Sea
so many years—
today your return
begins in China.

While absent from home,
your hair's turned white;
but at wave's end
blue hills will arise.

Separated by water,
we'll be in each other's thoughts;
but no letters
to distract your quiet life.

FAREWELL TO MASTER TAN RETURNING TO MIN

From Lo-yang's autumn willows
and cicadas,
your route is a lonely one
of whitecap and wave.

Your belongings will pass
through thunder and lightning;
at a spring on an island
you will wash before "sitting."

After long absence, you're
returning to your temple in the trees,
not putting ashore,
as you sail the coast of Yueh.

You say today is set
for your departure,
that you expect to grow old
by the sea.

送丹師歸閩中
波濤路杳然衰柳洛陽蟬
歸林久別寺過越未離船
行李經雷電禪前漱島泉
自說從今去身應老海邊

泥陽館

客愁何併起暮送故人回
廢館秋螢出空城寒雨來
夕陽飄白露樹影掃青苔
獨坐離容慘孤燈照不開

AT NI-YANG INN

A traveler's sadness,
how is it deepened?
By seeing off
an old friend at dusk.

At the tumbledown inn,
autumn fireflies are out;
in the empty town,
a cold rain comes.

The sun sets
in seasonal white dew;
tree shadows sweep
the green moss.

As I sit alone,
my mood after parting darkens;
the light of my single lamp
is weak.

THINKING OF RETIRED SCHOLAR WU ON THE RIVER

Since you set sail for the state of Min,
the moon has passed from full to full again.

Autumn wind arises on Wei River;
falling leaves fill Ch'ang-an.

I recall that evening together—
suddenly thunder, then cold rain.

Odd your orchidwood oar hasn't yet returned;
news of you ends at ocean clouds.

憶江上吳處士
閩國揚帆去蟾蜍虧復圓秋風生渭水落葉滿長安
此地聚會夕當時雷雨寒蘭橈殊未返消息海雲端

望水知柔性看山欲倦魂縱情猶未已迴馬欲黃昏　浩渺浸雲根煙嵐沒遠村鳥歸沙有跡帆過浪無痕　江亭晚望

LATE IN THE DAY, GAZING OUT
FROM A RIVER PAVILION

Water to the horizon
veils the base of clouds;
mountain mist
blurs the far village.

Returning to nest, birds
make tracks in the sand;
passing on the river, a boat
leaves no trace on the waves.

I gaze at the water
and know its gentle nature;
watch the mountains
until my spirit tires.

Though not yet ready
to leave off musing,
dusk falls,
and I return by horse.

AUSPICIOUS ARRIVAL OF YUNG T'AO

This morning
laughing together;
just a few such days
in a hundred.

After birds pass
over Sword Gate, it's calm;
invaders from the south
have withdrawn to the Lu River wilds.

We walk on frosted ground
praising chrysanthemums bordering fields
sit on the east edge of the woods,
waiting for the moon to rise.

Not having to be alone
is happiness;
we do not talk
of failure or success.

喜雍陶至
今朝笑語同幾日
百憂中鳥度劍門靜
蠻歸瀘水空
步霜吟菊畔待月坐林東
且莫孤此興勿論窮與通

送于總持歸京

別來二十一春風
出家初隷何方寺
上國西明御水東
卻見舊房皆下樹

SEEING OFF THE MONK TS'UNG-CH'IH
RETURNING TO THE CAPITAL

"When you left home
  to be a monk,
  to which temple
  did you first go?"

"Ch'ang-an's
  Western Light,
  east of the waters
  of the Palace Canal.

Going back, I'll see again
  the ancient buildings
  and, below the steps,
  the trees,

which, since I left,
  have known
  twenty-one winds
  of spring."

SPRING TRAVEL

Keeping on and on,
a traveler gets farther, farther away;
dust without cease
follows a horse through the world.

A traveler's feelings
after the sun's rays slant—
colors of spring
in the morning mist.

The river's flow heard
at the empty inn—
flowers just blooming
at the old palace.

I think of home
a thousand *li* away;
green-willow wind
stirs on the pond.

春行
去去行人遠塵隨馬不窮旅情斜日後春色早煙中
流水穿空館閒花發故宮舊鄉千里思池上綠楊風

Notes

Winter Night Farewell

▨ *Ch'u* was a large and powerful state that existed from 740–223 B.C.E. It occupied the middle Yangtze area in the south and stretched as far north as the upper reaches of the Huai River.

Memento on the Departure of a Friend

▨ *Yeh* was the ancient name for a part of what is today Honan Province.

▨ *Willows* are a symbol of parting.

Morning Travel

▨ The *bell* is a temple's dawn summons.

▨ Red Pine interprets this poem as being about Chia Tao's departure from monastic life: the "journey" is into the secular world; the "chickens" are the other monks; the innkeeper is the Ch'an master; the "slipping," the unsure footing of the poet; and the "daybreak," the daybreak.

Passing by a Mountain Village at Dusk

▨ A *li* is about one-third of a mile.

▨ *Border signal towers* employed lighted beacons to communicate between detachments guarding China's borders. Apparently, the poet is traveling outside *Ch'in*, the T'ang dynasty name for China.

Farewell to Monk Chih-hsing

▨ Although *Pa-hsing*, the temple, is not identified, a county of that name existed during the T'ang dynasty in Szechuan Province. *Sea*, or *hai*, can be any substantial expanse of water.

At I-chou, Climbing the Tower

▨ In T'ang times, the prefecture I-chou was located along the Szechuan-Hupei Road. Today, I-chou County lies within Hupei Province.

▨ *Lung-hsing Temple* is not identified.

Abode of the Unplanned Effect

▨ The *abode* was near or on the grounds of Sheng-tao Temple on a high plateau in a ward of the same name in southeast Ch'ang-an.

▨ The *Chungnan Mountains*, south of Ch'ang-an, are the divide of North and South China. The range stretches to the Chilien Mountains in the west, which in turn become the Kunlun Mountains extending to the border of northern India. In ancient times, this cordillera harbored China's shamans-turned-hermits, who earlier had lost temporal power to newly civilizing elements and had taken refuge in the mountains.

In the T'ang dynasty, the mountains were the home of sages who might be of any one or more of the seven or eight Buddhist schools, and of any number of Taoist sects as well. Even Confucianists had by then established a tradition of mountain retreat there.

▨ The person in the poem wears a *plain, white robe*; hence he is not a monk. *Pai-yi*, "white robe," often signals a sage.

▨ *Calming of the heart* is my translation for *wang chi*, or "forgetting schemes or designs in one's mind." *Wang-chi*, "forgetting self," is a Buddhist meditation practice.

A Farewell to T'ien Cho on Retreat

▨ *Hua Mountain*, located in Shensi Province, is one of the five sacred mountains of China.

▨ The *crane* is one of many symbols of longevity. Immortals were often depicted as flying on a crane's head or back.

Farewell to Master Tan Returning to Min

▨ *Min*, a Ten Kingdoms state, was roughly in the same area as present-day Fukien Province.

- *Lo-yang* was the summer, or eastern, capital for nearly three hundred years during the T'ang dynasty.
- *Yueh*, an ancient state of the Eastern Chou period (770–256 B.C.E.), included part of today's Chekiang Province.
- *Hsing-li*, translated here as *belongings*, is also the name of the Vinaya-vehicle, the teaching that emphasizes the rules of monastic conduct.

At Ni-yang Inn
- *Ni-yang* was a county seat north of Ch'ang-an.

Thinking of Retired Scholar Wu on the River
- Chia Tao indicates *the moon* by *ch'an ch'u*, or "the toad that lives in the moon."
- The couplet "Autumn wind arises on Wei River / Falling leaves fill Ch'ang-an" is famous in part for this anecdote: Chia Tao (as in the tale describing how he met Han Yu) was riding a donkey through the streets of Ch'ang-an, deeply absorbed in finding a parallel line to "Falling leaves fill Ch'ang-an." He found the line, but collided with a city official, who had him briefly jailed.
- *Wei River* flows east past Ch'ang-an in Shensi Province.
- *Orchidwood oar* signifies a boat.

Auspicious Arrival of Yung T'ao
- *Yung T'ao*, a native of Chengtu, the capital city of Szechuan, was a successful candidate of the Civil Service Examination who received the title of *po shih*, conferred upon scholars of profound learning.
- *Sword Gate*, or Chien-men Pass, is located in the Ta-chien mountains, in northern Szechuan.
- The *Lu River* is part of the upper reaches of the Yangtze River.

Seeing off the Monk Ts'ung-ch'ih
- *Western Light*, or *Hsi-ming*, was a temple near Ch'ang-an's South (Red Bird) Gate in the ward of Yen-k'ang.

Bibliography

EDITIONS OF CHIA TAO'S POETRY

Ch'ang-chiang chi. Ssu-pu pei-yao. Shanghai, 1927–1937; Rpt. Taipei, 1966.

Chia Ch'ang-chiang chi. Rpt. Taipei: China Books Co.

Ch'en, Yen-chieh, annotator and Yun-wu Wang, ed. *Chia Tao shih-chu*. Shanghai, 1937.

Ch'uan-T'ang-shih. Volume 2 (hsia). Rpt. Taipei: Hungyeh Book Company.

Hsu, Sung-po, ed. *Lu sheng-chih chi, Ch'ang-chiang chi ho-t'ing-pen*. Rpt. Taipei: Hsinan Book Co., 1973.

Liu, Ssu-han, ed. *Meng Chao Chia Tao shih-hsuan*. Rpt. Taipei, 1988.

TRANSLATIONS IN ENGLISH

Liu, Wu-chi and Irving Yu-cheng Lo, eds. *Sunflower Splendor: Three Thousand Years of Chinese Poetry*. Garden City, N.Y.: Anchor Press/ Doubleday, 1975.

O'Connor, Mike. *Colors of Daybreak and Dust: A Selection of Poems by Chia Tao*. Berkeley: Tangram Press, 1995.

O'Connor, Mike. *When I Find You Again, It Will Be in Mountains: Selected Poems of Chia Tao*. Berkeley: Tangram Press, 1996.

Owen, Stephen. "Some Mid-T'ang Quatrains." In *A Brotherhood in Song: Chinese Poetry and Poetics*, edited by Stephen C. Soong. Hong Kong: Chinese University Press, 1985.

Seaton, J.P. and Dennis Maloney, eds. *A Drifting Boat: An Anthology of Chinese Zen Poetry*. Fredonia, N.Y.: White Pine Press, 1994. (Several poems of Chia Tao under his religious name, Wu-pen (Wu Pen), translated by J.P. Seaton.)

Watson, Burton. "Buddhist Poet-Priests of the T'ang." In *The Eastern Buddhist* 25, no. 2 (1992): 30–58.

Studies

Chang, Yu-ming. "Ch'ang-chiang chi chiao-chu." Master's thesis, Kuo-li Shih-fan Ta-hsueh, 1969.

Li, Chia-yen. *Chia Tao nien-p'u*. Rpt. Taipei, 1974.

Witzling, Catherine. "The Poetry of Chia Tao: A Re-Examination of Critical Stereotypes." Ph. D. diss., Stanford University, 1980.

Note: Owing in part to its inclusion in the *T'ang-shih san-pai shou (Complete Poems of the T'ang)*, Chia Tao's poem "Seeking but Not Finding the Recluse" has numerous translators.

CH'I-CHI

Ch'i-chi (864–937)

Translations by Burton Watson

Introduction

CH'I-CHI IS ONE OF A GROUP of Buddhist monks that were active in poetry circles in the closing years of the T'ang dynasty, the other most prominent member of the group being Kuan-hsiu (832–912). They exchanged poems with many of the secular poets of the time, and their works influenced the development of Buddhist poetry in the centuries that followed.

Ch'i-chi, whose family name was Hu, was born in the Ch'ang-sha area of Hunan. Orphaned at an early age, he entered a nearby temple on Mount Ta-kuei, an important training center for monks of the Ch'an or Zen school, and in time became an ordained monk. Like many of the Ch'an monks of the period, he traveled around to other Buddhist centers. His name is associated in particular with Mount Heng in Hunan, and, as his poems reveal, he spent time in the Tung-lin-ssu temple at Mount Lu and the Kuo-ch'ing-ssu temple at Mount T'ien-t'ai. He also lived at one period in Ch'ang-an and acquainted himself with the Buddhist centers in the capital area.

When Ch'i-chi was young, China was beset by severe political and social turmoil as the T'ang dynasty faltered to a close. The rebellion led by Huang Ch'ao (d. 884) in particular devastated large areas of the country. In 907 T'ang rule ended when a military governor declared himself founder of a new dynasty known as the Posterior Liang. These troubled conditions and the hardships they inflicted on the population are alluded to in some of the poems that follow.

In 921 Ch'i-chi was invited by Kao Tsung-hui, military commissioner of the Chiang-ling area in Hupei, to head a temple called the Lung-hsing-ssu in Chiang-ling. In 928 Kao became ruler of an independent kingdom called Nan-p'ing, or Ching-nan, with his capital at Chiang-ling, and Ch'i-chi was apparently able to live the remainder of his life in Chiang-ling, associating with many of the eminent poet-officials of the time and enjoying wide recognition for his literary activities. In addition to poems, he wrote two brief critical works on poetry.

Ch'i-chi's poems are preserved in a work entitled *Pai-lien-chi,* or *The White Lotus Collection,* and are also found in chapters 838–847 of the *Ch'üan T'ang shih,* or *Complete T'ang Poetry.* The *Pai-lien-chi* is in ten chuan and contains about 820 poems. They do not appear to be arranged in any special order, though works of a satirical nature are for the most part grouped in the final chapter.

Most of Ch'i-chi's poems, as the titles indicate, were written in reply to poems from friends or to commemorate visits, farewell parties, or other social occasions. Some describe a particular scene or object in nature or deal with the poet's daily life, but there are very few works of an openly doctrinal nature.

Ch'i-chi wrote in the rather bland and low-key style favored by many poets of the late T'ang, a style modeled largely on that of Chia Tao (779–843), who spent the earlier years of his life as a Ch'an monk. Like the others of his group, he employs literary allusions sparingly and avoids any expression of intense emotion, aiming rather for an air of calmness and resignation.

As is common for writers in this style, Ch'i-chi's favors the eight-line *lu-shih,* or regulated verse form, which requires strict verbal parallelism in the two middle couplets, with a few poems in the four-line *chueh-chu* form. He also wrote a few works on *yueh-fu,* or folk song themes, in old poetry style in which he voiced criticisms of the moral and social ills of the time.

不睡

永夜不欲睡虛堂閉復開卻離燈影去待得月光來落
葉逢巢住飛螢值我迴天明拂經案一炷白檀灰

NOT SLEEPING

(5-character regulated verse, CTS 838)

Long night, no inclination to sleep,
empty hall, opening and shutting doors:
deliberately I move out of the glow of the lamp,
wait where I'll catch the moonlight when it comes.
Falling leaves suspended, snagged in a bird's nest,
streams of fireflies circling round me—
at dawn I dust off the sutra stand,
sandalwood ash from one stick of incense.

SENT TO A POETRY FRIEND

*(5-character regulated verse, CTS 838. In line two the term k'u-hsin,
"laboring mind," refers in particular to the process of poetic composition.
Ch'i-chi and his contemporaries liked to emphasize how hard they worked
at writing poetry.)*

Ten thousand things in heaven and earth—
all should be fodder for the laboring mind.
Though others would like to understand,
this Way of Poetry is profound indeed!
Returning to simplicity, you ignore current happenings,
shut your gate, getting through the year-end.
I thought of you these past fall evenings,
both of us facing the cold lamp, composing.

天地有萬物盡應輸苦心
他人雖欲解此道奈何深
返朴遺時態關門度歲陰
相思去秋夕共對冷燈吟

自髮

莫染亦莫鑷任從伊滿頭白雖無耐藥黑也不禁秋靜

枕聽蟬臥閒垂看水流浮生未遠此多爲爾爲愁

WHITE HAIR
(5-character regulated verse, CTS 838)

Don't dye it, don't pull it out,
let it grow all over your head.
No medicine can stop the whiteness,
the blackness won't last out the fall.
Lay your head on a quiet pillow, hear the cicadas,
idly incline it to watch the waters flow—
The reason we can't rise to this broader view of life
is because, white hair, you grieve us so!

LITTLE PINES

(5-character regulated verse, CTS 840)

Poking up from the ground barely above my knees,
already there's holiness in their coiled roots.
Though harsh frost has whitened the hundred grasses,
deep in the courtyard, one grove of green!
In the late night long-legged spiders stir;
crickets are calling from the empty stairs.
A thousand years from now who will stroll
   among these trees,
fashioning poems on their ancient dragon shapes?

小松

發地纏過膝蟠根已有靈嚴霜百草白深院一株青後

夜蕭騷動空階蟋蟀聽誰於千歲外吟遠老龍形

難多戰地野闊絕春耕骨肉知存否林園近郡城

風濤出洞庭帆影入澄清何處驚鴻起孤舟趁月行時

夜次湘陰

STOPPING AT NIGHT AT HSIANG-YIN

(5-character regulated verse, CTS 841. Written when the poet was on his way by boat from Mount Heng to Ching-chou and was stopping at Hsiang-yin on Lake Tung-t'ing in Hunan, near his old home in Ch'ang-sha.)

Wind and waves rising on Lake Tung-t'ing,
the sail's reflection cast over clear waters:
somewhere a startled swan flies up
as our lone boat chases the moon.
I see so many sites these days where battles raged,
broad-stretching fields but no trace of spring planting.
And what of my kin—do they still exist,
and the groves of home near this country town?

50

ON AN AUTUMN EVENING
LISTENING TO REVEREND YEH PLAY THE CH'IN

(5-character regulated verse, CTS 841. The ch'in, a zither-like stringed instrument played in horizontal position, symbolizes the morally uplifting music of antiquity.)

The ten thousand things all hushed and silent,
intent upon hearing these upright tones—
when human hearts are all like this,
then the world will be at peace.
Hsiang waters pouring forth autumn blue,
ancient winds blowing across the great void—
I heard them long ago when you played on Mt. Lu;
this evening I discover them again.

秋夜聽業上人彈琴
萬物都寂寂堪聞彈正聲人心盡如此天下自和平湘
水瀉秋碧古風吹太清往年盧岳奏今夕更分明

秋夕寄諸姪

每到秋殘夜燈前憶故鄉園林紅橘柚窗戶碧瀟湘離

別身垂老艱難路去長弟兄應健在兵火裏耕桑

AUTUMN EVENING:
TO SEND TO MY NIECES AND NEPHEWS
*(5-character regulated verse, CTS 841. The poet
writing to his relatives in his old home in Ch'ang-sha.)*

Each year, come the late autumn evenings,
I sit by the lamp recalling my old home,
gardens and groves red with oranges and pomelos,
windows and doors blue with Hsiao and Hsiang waters.
But since I left you old age has come on,
I quail at the long road that parts us.
Brothers young and old, just so you're well,
tending fields and silkworms amid these fires of war!

THINKING OF A MONK OF FLOWER SUMMIT
ON MOUNT T'IEN-T'AI

(5-character regulated verse, CTS 842. Flower Summit is the highest peak in the T'ien-t'ai Mountains, a range overlooking the ocean in Chekiang that is noted for its Buddhist and Taoist temples. Stone Bridge and the waterfall beneath it are natural features of the mountains, often mentioned in poetry. Kuo-ch'ing-ssu, at the foot of the range, is the main Buddhist temple in the area. The Wise One (Chih-chi) is the famous Buddhist monk and philosopher Chih-i (538–597), the virtual founder of the T'ien-t'ai school of Buddhism. His stupa is located halfway up the mountain.)

Flower Summit precipitous, overlooking the sea,
Stone Bridge enveloped in rosy sunset—
once from Kuo-ch'ing Temple
I climbed up to gaze at moon-bright tides.
Kindly birds drew close to my incense and lamp;
the wild stream jetted into empty air.
I wish I could go again, make the Wise One my teacher,
but my head is white and the road so very long.

懷天台華頂僧
華頂危臨海丹霞裛石橋曾從國清寺上看月明潮好
鳥親香火狂泉噴沈寥欲歸師智者頭白路迢迢

病起見閑雲

石終無跡從風或有聞仙山足鸞鳳歸去自同群
病起見閑雲空中聚又分滯留堪笑我舒卷不如君觸

UP AFTER ILLNESS, I WATCH THE IDLE CLOUDS
(5-character regulated verse, CTS 842)

Up after illness, I watch the idle clouds
crowding together in the sky, then parting,
pausing long enough to laugh at me—
I could never match your twists and turnings!
Colliding with rocks, you leave no trace;
obeying the wind, you seem to have ears.
This mountain of the immortals has phoenixes enough—
better be off to flock with your own kind.

QUIETLY DISCUSSING MY THOUGHTS
WITH THE COLLATOR OF TEXTS TS'UI

(7-character regulated verse, CTS 844. Nothing is known of the poet's friend Ts'ui except what the poem tells us, namely that he held the rather low official post of collator of texts.)

Both born in the same year of the Hsien-t'ung era,[1]
one serving Buddha, one a Confucian, highest of aims.
It's my nature—I'm content to wear these robes
    of the patriarch,
though at heart you still wait the day you can doff
    your blue official's gown.
Frosty whiskers—how many times do you consult
    the bronze mirror at dawn?[2]
Snowy locks, thin with the cold, they fall before my razor.
Withdrawal from the world, audience with the
    sovereign—neither of us got that far,
but no harm if we exchange these greetings in rhyme.

與崔拔書靜話言懷

同年生在咸通裏事佛爲儒趣盡高我性已甘披祖衲
君心猶待脫藍袍霜髭曉幾臨銅鏡雪鬢寒疏落剃刀
出世朝天俱未得不妨還往有風騷

亂後經西山寺

松燒寺砍是刀兵谷變陵遷事可驚雲裏乍逢新住主

石邊重認舊題名閑臨菡萏荒池坐亂踏鴛鴦砍瓦行

欲伴高僧重結社此身無計捨前程

AFTER THE REBELLION,
VISITING WEST MOUNTAIN TEMPLE
(7-character regulated verse, CTS 845)

Pines charred, temple wrecked, all from the fighting;
valleys transformed, ridges shifted—unbelievable
    events![3]
Among clouds I suddenly meet the new head priest;
on the rocks I spy inscriptions from earlier visits.
Idly I sit peering at a ruined pond where lotuses
    bloomed,
pick my way over broken tiles of a once neatly
    patterned walk.
I hope to join these fine monks in mending ties;
I for one have no plans to abandon the road I'm on.

THE YEAR KENG-WU, NIGHT OF
THE FIFTEENTH, FACING THE MOON

(7-character chueh-chu, CTS 847. The Keng-wu year is 910,
three years after the overthrow of the T'ang and the establishment
of the Posterior Liang dynasty. Emperor Hsuan-tsung (r. 712–755)
was the ruler whose reign marked the height of T'ang culture and
whose follies helped lead to the long decline and downfall of the
dynasty and the destruction of its capital, Ch'ang-an.)

Sea calm, sky blue, moon just now full—
in my poems I think how cold Hsuan-tsung must
    be tonight.
The jade rabbit in the moon, if he has a heart, will
    remember too,
as he looks west and cannot see the old Ch'ang-an.

庚午歲十五夜對月
海澄空碧正團圓吟想玄宗此夜寒玉兔有情應記得
西邊不見舊長安

爾本青山一衲白石孤禪今王侯搆室安之
給俸食之使之樂然萬事都外游息自得則雲泉
猿鳥不必爲狎其放縱若是夫何繫乎

DON'T ASK

("Don't Ask" is a series of fifteen poems in five-character regulated verse form, all of which begin with the words mo wen, or "don't ask." The series was written in 921 when the poet was appointed to head a temple called Lung-hsing-ssu in Chiang-ling, Hupei. The appointment was made by Kao Tsung-hui, the military commissioner of the area. In a brief introduction to the series, Ch'i-chi describes his new appointment by saying: "Originally I was a monk of the green mountains, sitting in solitary meditation on a white rock. But now these noblemen have built rooms to house me, provided funds to feed me, and arranged for my complete comfort. Relieved of all the ten thousand concerns, at liberty to roam or rest as I choose, I hence no longer need keep company with the clouds and springs, the wild monkeys and birds. If I can be as carefree as this, what could there be to tie me down?")

DON'T ASK

(5-character regulated verse, CTS 842, first in the series)

Don't ask if I'm out of touch with human affairs:
kings, marquises—I leave all to them now.
Boorish by nature, no harm if I let it show,
the way I did when I lived in the mountains.
In quiet moments I enter the soundless music,
in my madness reject properly ordered poems.
I act for myself, look after myself,
hoping the man in charge will understand.

入無聲樂狂拋正律詩自爲仍自愛敢望至公知

莫問疏人事王侯已任伊不妨隨野性還似在山時靜

莫問關門意從來寡往還道應歸淡泊身合在空閒四
面苔圍綠窗兩洒斑夢尋何處去秋色水邊山

DON'T ASK

(Fifth in the series)

Don't ask why I shut my gate—
from times past, few comings and goings.
The Way should rest in simplicity,
the body's best suited to vacant idleness.
On four sides green moss surrounds me,
my lone window dotted with rain spatters.
And where do dream-wanderings take me?
To where autumn is coloring the riverside hills.

DON'T ASK

(Ninth in the series)

Don't ask if I've ceased my wanderings—
already I've tramped all over the south.
Understanding should be what you yourself understand;
mind is not someone else's mind!
Why search for the Red Water pearl?
Stop composing those Cold Mountain *gathas*![4]
With whom can I discuss this philosophy?
I'll be silent, since so few can follow my tune.

莫問休行腳南方已遍尋了應須自了心不是他心赤
水珠何覓寒山偈莫吟誰同論此理杜口少知音

莫問無求意浮雲喻可知滿盈如不戒倚伏更何疑樂
矣賢顏子窮乎聖仲尼已過知命歲休把運行推

DON'T ASK
(Eleventh in the series)

Don't ask if I've ceased wanting anything—
we all know the simile of the drifting clouds.[5]
Excess wouldn't fit the precepts:
take what comes and you're never in doubt.
How happy, that worthy Yen![6]
Even the sage Confucius was poor.
Once you've passed the age of understanding[7]
stop trying to change destiny's course.

EARLY PLUM BLOSSOMS

(5-character regulated verse, CTS 843)

Ten thousand trees frozen, just about to crack,
this lone tree only, warm, reviving:
in the village nearby, deep in snow,
last night one branch came into bloom.[8]
Breezes waft the hidden fragrance,
birds come seeking the white beauty of blossoms.
Next year again, if it's true to season,
first to shed brightness over the spring terrace!

早梅

萬木凍欲折孤根暖迴前村深雪裏昨夜一枝開風
遞幽香去禽窺素艷來明年猶應律先發映春臺

63

新秋病中枕上聞蟬
枕上稍醒醒忽聞蟬一聲此時知不死昨日即前生更
欲臨窗聽猶難策杖行尋應同蛻殼重飲露華清

START OF AUTUMN:

HEARING A CICADA WHILE SICK IN BED

(5-character regulated verse, CTS 843)

On my pillow bit by bit waking,
suddenly I hear a cicada cry—
at that moment I know I've not died,
though past days are like a former existence.
I want to go to the window, listen closer,
but even with a cane I can't manage.
Before long like you I'll shed my shell
and drink again the clear brightness of the dew.[9]

SPEAKING MY MIND

(7-character regulated verse, CTS 846)

Poetry sickness makes the old-age sickness
    even worse;
with the best of physicians I'd still pay out
    huge sums in vain.
In life's remnant, why must I give it up for nothing?
Before I die, what harm if I amuse myself
    writing poems?
Flowing waters never return—save your sighs;
white clouds leave no trail—don't try to chase them!
An idle man knows where to while away idleness:
yellow leaves, fresh breeze, a grove full of cicadas.

遣懷

詩病相兼老病深世醫徒更費千金餘生豈必虛拋擲

未死何妨樂詠吟流水不迴休歎息白雲無跡莫追尋

閑身自有閑消處黃葉清風蟬一林

喜乾畫上人遠相訪

彼此垂七十相逢意若何聖明殊未至離亂更應多
泊門難到從容日易過餘生消息外只合聽詩魔

DELIGHTED THAT THE MONK CH'IEN-CHOU
HAS COME A LONG WAY TO VISIT ME
(5-character regulated verse, CTS 839)

He and I both nearing seventy,
what does it mean to meet like this?
The age of a sage king has yet to arrive,
but partings and rebellions—we have plenty of that!
Though the gate to detachment is hard to attain,
days of leisure pass quickly.
For the rest of our lives, aside from writing letters,
we'll just be at the beck of the poetry devil.[10]

THE OLD FARMER

(5-character regulated verse, CTS 847)

Spring winds buffet his straw cape,
twilight rain wets his bamboo hat,
husband and wife working the land together,
young ones nearby, crying with hunger.
Their fields are steep and rocky,
taxes heavy, payments due—
granary officials are so many rats and sparrows,
just waiting for new levies to come in!

耕叟

春風吹蓑衣暮雨滴篛笠夫婦耕共勞兒孫饑對泣田

園高且瘦賦稅重復急官倉鼠雀群只待新租入

輕薄行

玉鞭金鐙驊騮蹄橫眉吐氣如霓五陵春曖芳草齊

笙歌到處花成泥日沉月上且鬥雞醉來草問天高低

伯陽道德何唾咦仲尼禮樂徒卑栖

SONG OF THE INSOLENT AIR

(7-character yueh-fu *style, CTS 847.*
A satire on the rich young men of the capital area.)

Jade whips, gold stirrups, hooves of a thoroughbred;
surly glances, breath coming out like rainbows.[11]
In the Five Towns spring is warm, fragrant grasses thriving;[12]
pipes, songs everywhere, blossoms gone to mud.
The sun sets, the moon rises—now for the cockfights—
once drunk, who cares if Heaven is high or low?
Lao-tzu's Way and Power—something to spit on;
Confucius's rites and music—fit for servants and menials!

SONG OF THE OLD SWORD

(7-character old style, CTS 847)

Ancient men with their hands forged this
    wondrous object,
a hundred firings, a hundred baths in water,
    till it was finished.
Men of today need not labor to hone and polish—
tip and blade have never lost their starry markings.
With each thrust, each flourish, we hear its clanging cry;
the old dragon's gleam outshines the autumn lamps.
When will you meet with a master of heroic mold
who can wield you to bring peace to the realm?

古劍歌

古人手中鑄神物
百錬百淬始提出
今人不要強硎磨
蓮鍔星文未曾沒
一彈一撫聞錚錚
老龍影奪秋燈明
何時得遇英雄主
用爾平治天下去

69

春風曲

春風有何情旦暮來林園不問桃李主吹落紅無言

SONG OF THE SPRING WIND
(5-character chueh-chu, *CTS 847)*

What does the spring wind have in mind,
coming day and night to these groves and gardens?
It never asks who owns the peach and damson trees
but blows away their crimson without a word.

ADMONISHING A YOUNGER TEACHER

(7-character chueh-chu, *CTS 847)*

You decline to write poetry, won't listen to sutras,
too lazy to visit the other peaks of Ch'an—
when at last your head is white and they question you,
what stories will you have to tell your students?

戒小師

不肯吟詩不聽經
禪宗異岳懶遊行
他年白首當人問
將底言談對後生

夏日城中作二首
三面僧鄰一面牆更無風路可吹涼他年捨此歸何處
青壁紅霞裏石房

WRITTEN ON A SUMMER DAY IN THE CITY
(7-character chueh-chu, *CTS 847. The first of two poems
with this title.)*

Monk neighbors on three sides, a wall on the fourth,
no passage for the wind to blow me a puff of cool—
if some year I left here, where would I go?
To a cell of stone among blue cliffs and red sunset skies.

Notes

1. The years 860–873.

2. Government officials had to report for duty very early in the morning.

3. Metaphorical reference to the violent political upheavals of the time.

4. According to *Chuang-tzu*, sec. 12, in ancient times the Yellow Emperor lost his Dark Pearl while wandering in the region of Red Water. The following line is probably a reference to the kind of *gathas*, or Buddhist hymns, written by the poet Han-shan, the Master of Cold Mountain.

5. In *Analects* VII, 16, Confucius declared that wealth and rank gained through unjust means were no more to him than drifting clouds.

6. Yen Hui, Confucius's favorite disciple, who knew how to be content even in poverty.

7. In *Analects* II, 4, Confucius said that at the age of fifty he "understood the Mandate of Heaven."

8. It is said that Ch'i-chi's fourth line originally read "last night several branches came into bloom." When he showed the poem to his friend, the poet-official Cheng Ku, the latter remarked that if several branches were already in bloom, the blossoms were not really "early." He therefore suggested that the character for "several" be changed to "one." People of the time so admired

73

this emendation that Cheng Ku became known as the "One Character Teacher."

9. According to Chinese belief the cicada subsists entirely on dew and hence epitomizes the life of purity.

10. The T'ang poet Po Chu-i (772–846), a dedicated Buddhist, jokingly described his addiction to poetry writing as a form of possession by what he dubbed the "poetry devil."

11. Indicative of the high-spirited nature of the young men.

12. The Five Towns were towns established in Han times at the site of imperial tombs in the suburbs of Ch'ang-an; they came to symbolize the lifestyle of the wealthy.

Poetic Minds Complete
the Greater Elegance:
The Nine Monks and Chih Yuan,
Poet Monks of Early Sung China
(late tenth century)

Translations by Paul Hansen

INTRODUCTION

IN THE EARLY DECADES of the Sung dynasty, nine Buddhist monks from widely separate areas in China, attracted by their mutual interest in poetry, sent poems back and forth, visited one another for small poetry gatherings, played music together, and probably traveled in one another's company. Some of them were acquainted with notable officials and hermits of the times, for we find mention of K'ou Chun and poems addressed to Ting Wei, Ch'ung Fang, Lin Pu, and Wei Yeh. Beyond those interested in the poetry of monks, only one of the circle, Hui Ch'ung, achieved recognition for his small landscape paintings.

Very early in the eleventh century a selection of their poems was made, called *Poems of the Nine Monks*, although the poet monks themselves may never have used that collective name. The *Poems of the Nine Monks*, a small volume of 135 poems, was already hard to find a few decades after the monks vanished from the scene around 1010. It experienced a precarious existence for several hundred years until it was reprinted in 1787 and reprinted again in the great collections of this century.

Beyond their very general areas of origin, what we know about the monks themselves is only what their poems tell us. Though aspects of the Late T'ang style, in which they crafted their work, were already being discarded for something new in poetry, the poems of these monks remain crisp and well crafted. Indeed their diction, in the tradition of hermit poets, is appropriately "rugged," i.e., the word order is challenging, unusual, and potentially ambiguous. However, I feel it is their ultimate literary attainment that in their accomplished poetry these monks offer intense and non-dogmatic insights into moments of Buddhist life from the perspective of those traditionally central to it.

We do know something more about Chih Yuan. A native of Hangzhou, he was born in 976 and became an apprentice-monk at the age of seven, when he "left home" (a Buddhist term meaning to leave the secular life and enter the order of monks and nuns) at the Lung-hsing Monastery in that city. In his youth he made notable progress in his study and application of the teachings of the T'ien-t'ai School of Chinese Buddhism. Later he was abbot of Mao-nao Monastery on Ku-shan Island in West Lake, just outside the city. There, he and the cultivated Taoist hermit Lin Pu became friends and probably exchanged poems, though none of the latter's poems to Chih Yuan remain today.

Chih Yuan was well read in traditional Chinese philosophy and literature as well as the scriptures of Buddhism, and many poems in his collection arose from his extra-canonical studies. Other than Buddhist practice, study, and writing poetry, he actively pursued his duties as abbot of Mao-nao Monastery and made a number of improvements there. In 1022, after gathering his disciples together and composing a final Buddhist verse for them, the noted abbot passed away. Like the work of his colleagues the Nine Monks, Chih Yuan's collection of poems experienced vicissitudes and has not been independently preserved; the remainder, though, a collection of eleven *chuan*, is in the Japanese *Continuation of the Tripitika*, and, like that of the Nine Monks, has been reprinted in the *Complete Sung Poetry*.

The ability of these monks in poetry led to their being called *poetry monks*, a term some might employ in a disparaging sense. Yet from earliest times spontaneous verses have always been a part of the Buddhist tradition. The stanza concluding the *Diamond Sutra* offers a superb example:

As stars, a fault of vision, as a lamp,
    A mock show, dew drops, or a bubble,

A dream, a lightning flash, or cloud
So should one view what is conditioned

In a tradition of spiritual poetry and at a great distance of time
and culture it is frequently these immediate revelations of language
that bring the experiences of earlier Buddhists, august and humble,
to us most vividly today: the other-worldly truths of the *Diamond
Sutra*, or a monk washing his clothes. As the Monk Wei Feng points
out in defense of the art for Buddhists:

Poetic
   Minds complete
   The Greater Elegance. The intent
   Of the patriarchs employs every method.

I would like to take the pleasurable opportunity to thank all those
who helped me with this project. The late Professor Hellmut Wil-
helm, who first pointed out the work of the Nine Monks to me;
Professor Maureen Robertson, Bill Porter, and Michael O'Connor,
who have seen parts of the present work at various stages; Sam and
Sally Green, who published an earlier selection of my translations
from the Nine Monks; Paul Hunter, whose shared insights made
significant improvements on the final draft; and my wife Jennifer
Clarke, for her constant help and warm support in these curious
efforts.

BROKEN TABLETS

A slice
Of precious stone
The pressing cold has split.
In the fallen script
I see broken bugs.

Sinking
At a distance
On the hill's grass edge, or half-revealed
In an icy stream, deeds writ down, how
Could the people exist? Years
Melted away, their affairs
Already empty.

I only hear
Cypress on the wrecked
Mound mourn together,
As the grieving wind
Rises.

Hsi Chou

斷碑

片玉侵寒折零文見斷蟲遠沉岡草際半露塹冰中

跡著人何在年銷事已空惟聞壞陵柏相弔起悲風

寄懷古

見說鵰陰僻人煙半雜羌
樹勢分孤壘河流出遠荒遙知林下客吟苦夜禪忘

見說鵰陰僻人煙半雜羌秋深邊日短風勁曉笳長

SENT
TO HUAI KU

Hearsay
You've hid out
Around T'iao-yin, where Chinese
And Ch'iang cook-smoke
Half-merge.

Autumn
Gets deeper, the border
Day shortens, wind stronger,
The dawn piping long. Wooded terrain
Splits around a single rampart,
The river current rises
On a distant steppe.

Far off
I know the traveler
Who visited our grove
Chants hard-wrought poems,
Forgot with Zen
At night.

Hsi Chou

FAREWELL TO WEI FENG,
GOING TO FAR-SOUTH MOUNTAIN

Inside the Pass
The freeze, arriving early,
Half-withers South Mountain's
Myriad trees.

In long space,
Human prospects are extreme.
Alone, as snow drifts up, you watch
The distance. The work of *Quiet Breathing*
Precludes fellow hermits. Chanting idle
Rhymes, you neglect to carry
Firewood.

Peak-tip
Moon pressing tight,
Remembrance rises
In the night.

Hsi Chou

送惟鳳之終南山
關內寒生早南山萬木凋長空人望絕積雪獨尋遙
靜息非同隱閒吟忽背樵幾侵峰頂月想念起中宵

早春闕下寄觀公

客心長念隱早晚解書招看月前期阻論山靜會遙

微陽生遠道殘雪下中宵坐見青門柳依依又結條

EARLY SPRING
AT THE CAPITAL,
SENT TO THE HONORABLE KUAN

A wanderer's mind
Constantly recalls seclusion.
Early this morning I got
Your invitation.

Our date
To watch the Moon
Has problems. A quiet visit
To discuss the mountains is far off.
On a distant road scant sunlight
Grows. By midnight
The final snow
Will fall.

Sitting, I see
The willows by Blue Gate,
Soft-softly sprout again
New sprigs.

Hsi Chou

AUTUMN PATH

Fir, bamboo,
And pure shade merge.
As I stroll, the mind
Has inclinations.

A chill
Springs up just
When rain has passed.
As stillness stretches out, monks
Suddenly return. Bug tracks wind
Into obscure holes. Moss
Traces connect broken
Eave corners.

My thoughts
Turn to a place
Of deep reclusion,
Down from the summit
Ridge after ridge.

Pao Hsien

秋徑

杉竹青陰合閒行
蟲跡穿幽穴苔痕接斷稜翻思深隱處峰頂下層層
意有憑涼生初過雨靜極忽歸僧

惟鳳師壁
書

草徑通深院秋來心更閒城中無舊識門外是他山

究寂生吟思持齋得病顏寒宵多約我靜話出人間

WRITTEN
ON THE WALL
AT MASTER WEI FENG'S

The grassy path
Leads to a deep cloister.
Arriving in Autumn
Eases my heart
Even more.

In town
No one I've known long.
Outside the gate, another mountain.
Exploring the silence gives poetic
Thought birth. Fasting
Confers a sick look.

On freezing nights
You arrange to meet me often:
Silent talk beyond
Human space.

Pao Hsien

SENT
TO YUAN CHEN
AT WHITE CABIN PEAK

I heard once
You've returned to White Cabin,
Not entering Ch'ang-an
Again.

A topmost
Peak lacks any people
Higher. The west wind pierces
All night: chillier. You ride the snow
To pass a hanging cliff,
Cross a cloud to watch
The torrent spew.

Remember
The fame gallopers. It's hard
For them to find the road
Among blue
Clouds.

Pao Hsien

寄白閣元貞
一聞歸白閣更不入長安絕頂無人上西風徹夜寒
懸崖乘雪度飛瀑過雲看應念馳名者青雲得路難

巴峽聞猿

倚棹望雲際寥寥出峽清心如無一事愁不在三聲

帶露諸峰迴懸空片月明何人同此聽徹曉得詩成

HEARING
THE GIBBONS CALL
IN PA GORGE

As I lean
On my oar, gazing
At the cloud-line, purity
Emerges, deep and lonely,
From the Gorge.

When the mind
Doesn't have anything
On it, there's no sorrow
Inherent in repeated calls. They bear
The dew where every peak is distant,
Dangle in space where a slice
Of Moon shines
Bright.

Whoever
Hears it like this
Can finish a poem
By dawn.

Wen Chao

FAREWELL
TO MASTER YU CHAO

We meet
To part again.
I have no words to respond
To this double
Inspiration.

Light snow
Falls on every peak.
A single monk walks
Along the only road. You strike your chime
Through a smoky village, begging noon rice,
And spark the lamp in a stone room,
Chanting poems at night.

Elsewhere,
A chapter of monks
Has asked you to come and live,
Continuing the lineage
Of the southerner,
Hui-neng.

Wen Chao

送宇昭師

相見又相別無言感倍興諸峰微下雪一路獨行僧
午飯煙村磬宵吟石屋燈他方人請住又得繼南能

87

聽宇昭師琴

遙空雨初霽深徑蟬未鳴忽品文王弦若聽宣尼聲

月色半峰出秋光四簷清韻斷意轉冥塵心若爲情

LISTENING
TO MASTER YU CHAO
PLAY THE LUTE

Far space
As rain first stops,
A deep path, where cicadas
Still haven't started
Keening.

Suddenly
There's a passage
Of the plaintive *King Wen Rhythm*,
Like hearing music made by Master K'ung.
Half up the peak, a lunar color emerges.
Under the eaves of heaven,
Autumn light
Pure.

As
The resonance
Stops, the final turn
Is quiet and profound. A dusty
Heart cannot feel
The feeling.

Heng Chao

FAREWELL
TO VINAYA MASTER TS'UNG,
TRAVELING IN THE WEST

Coiled, scaly
Dragons, awaiting spring
Renewal, watch the distant sky,
Seeking warm weather for their return.
Frightened birds leave an old nest
Thoughts distant,
Flight lagging.

It's sad the times
Ignore your urgent, solitary will.
The world little listens to the lute-strings
Of the heart. Thoughtful reflection rare,
Even in antiquity. Emerging from the Pass,
You'll carry your own baggage. Entering
Ch'in, on whose door
Will you knock?

If you suddenly lose
Your dusty eye, out of the distance
The rainstorm will gradually lessen,
And you'll see a rainbow dart out,
Striking the Immortals Palm
With a cold light.

Heng Chao

送從律師西遊

蟄鱗伺新春，望極融融歸。
驚禽別舊巢，念遠遲遲飛。
吁君腹至業，歲故志獨違。
心弦世寡聽，意鑑古亦稀。
出關自荷篋，入秦扣誰扉。
埃目若忽失，風雨遠漸微。
將看吐虹章，冷射仙掌輝。

贈峽山清倫師

褰衣汲靈水混滌巾履塵煙靄霽杉竹澄凝此心神

高僧灑眞雨澤彼寒草春華月寫空印清霜肅齋身

猶言振金策歸作耶溪鄰

GIVEN
TO MASTER CH'ING-LUN
OF HSIA MOUNTAIN

Pulling up
My robes, I draw magic water
From the spring and let it surge,
To scrub clogs and headcloth. Smoky
Haze breaking over fir and bamboo,
Clears and concentrates
The mind and spirit.

A lofty
Monk, you scatter
The true rain that annoints a springtime
Of frozen grass. Under a splendid Moon
You write the seal of emptiness,
In the pure frost your fasting
Body withers.

If you
Still talk of rattling
The brass on your walking staff around,
Come back and be a neighbor
At Ye Creek.

Chien Chang

SENT
TO ZEN MASTER YUN-SHUI

A thousand
Peaks arise in cold azure.
The ancient abbey disregards
The autumn clouds.

A lofty man,
You've halted
Your obscure traces.
What reason could there be for you
To hear of worldly things? On a Zen rock
You embrace blue moss, in patriarch's
Robes retain a clear,
Auspicious air.

Sometimes
You walk down the creek
Alone, with a crowd
Of birds and apes.

Chien Chang

寄雲水禪師
千峰聳寒翠古剎凌秋雲高人欲幽跡世事何由聞
禪石抱蒼蘚祖衣含淨氣有時溪上步自與鳥猿群

STAYING
WITH MASTER HENG CHAO
AT ROOST OF THE SAGES MONASTERY
ON MOUNT LU

與行肇師宿廬山棲賢寺

冰瀑寒侵室圍鑪靜話長詩心全大雅祖意會諸方

磬斷危杉月燈殘古塔霜無眠向遙夕又約去衡陽

The waterfall
Is frozen. Cold presses
In the room. Around the stove
Our quiet talk
Lasts long.

Poetic
Minds complete
The Greater Elegance. The intent
Of the patriarchs employs every method.
Chimes stop: Moon over steep fir.
Lamplight dwindles: frost
On the ancient
Tower.

Not sleepy
The long night, we agree
Again we'll be going
To Heng-yang.

Wei Feng

GIVEN
TO WEN CHAO

Staying by chance
At a monastery in the capital,
Who found who again?
To wander around
Together.

A solitary crane
Watches the dawn lecture.
Neighbor monks listen to a night-time
Lute. For filling jugs the gravel well
Is far; to ring a chime
The snowy chamber,
Deep.

Long parted
From pine trees and vines,
My mind hangs in space
Around King's Chamber
Mountain.

Hui Ch'ung

贈文兆

偶依京寺住誰復得相尋獨鶴窺朝講鄰僧聽夜琴

注瓶沙井遠鳴磬雪房深久與松蘿別空懸王屋心

松柄
澗底分貞幹寧將塵尾同坐間長滴翠話次忽生風
影落孤燈外聲寒靜室中有誰知此意林下石叢叢

THE PINE WHISK

A streambed
Winds between their solid trunks.
How could they be the same
As deertail fly-whisks?

To sit
Among them,
They're always dripping
Azure shade, and when we talk,
Give sudden birth to breezes. Their shadows
Fall beyond the lonely lamplight.
Noises chill inside
The silent room.

Is there anyone
Who realizes this thought?
The rocks in the woods,
Clustered together.

Yü Chao

LIVING
ON THE PLAIN
IN EARLY AUTUMN

Autumn's born
Along a deep path.
Old and sick, my eyes
Open lazy.

Outside
My door the monks
Have vanished. In the woods
A north wind plays. Chaotic crickets
Call from an ancient moat. Lingering
Sunlight illuminates
A desolate terrace.

But
There's a date
On another mountain
Close friends coming
In sight.

Huai Ku

原居早秋
秋生深徑裏老病眼慵開戶外行人絕林閒朔吹回
亂蛩鳴古塹殘日照荒臺惟有他山約相親入望來

寺居寄簡長

雪苑東山寺山深少往還紅塵無夢想白日自安閒

杖履苔花上香燈樹影閒何須更飛錫歸隱沃洲山

LIVING AT A MONASTERY,
SENT TO CHIEN CHANG

Snow collects
On East Mountain Monastery.
Deep in the mountains few people
Come and go.

Without daydreams
About red dust, in the pale sun
I'm peacefully at ease, or among moss
And flowers with a staff and clogs,
Or in the wooded shadow
Near an incense lamp.

What's
The need to fly away
On your walking stick again?
Come back as a recluse
To Mount Wo-chou.

Huai Ku

ROTTEN
AXE-HANDLE
MOUNTAIN

I.

At the Immortals' Home
They make light of the year or month,
While the passing night and day
Weigh down the Floating World.
White hair has *before* and *after*.
Green mountains no ancient
Or now.

Game over,
The axe-handle's rotten,
Dust dispersed, the sea still deep.
Seeking the road to Long Life
Where do you look among mist
And sun-tinted clouds?

II.

In the matter
Of Wang Chih
And his rotten axe-handle,
There's no doubting what we hear
In the tradition. It was easy
To visit for a hundred years.
The game waiting
For an idle stone
To move.

Who saw
The move? Nothing being said,

爛柯山二首

仙家輕歲月
浮世重光陰
白髮有先後
青山無古今
局終柯已爛
塵散海尤深
若覓長生路
煙霞無處尋

王質爛柯事
傳聞不在疑
百年容易客
一局等閒棋
此著有誰見
無言祇自知
石橋南畔路
依舊日斜暉

Only I myself know it. South Border Road
To Stonebridge Mountain,
In slanting sunlight
As of old.

Huai Ku

LIVING
IN POVERTY

The stove
In my mountain kitchen
Is tracked with blue moss.
Dust fills the almsbowl.
There isn't any food.

A pity
Mice and sparrows
Haven't learned about poverty yet,
Drilling into the room, drilling
Through the walls.

Chih Yuan

穿屋穿墉不暫息
山廚竈上苔痕碧齋盂生塵無粒食可憐雀鼠未知貧
貧居

詠亡有禪師山齋養獼猴

閒庭樹菓垂霜聽法猶憐入草堂異類豈能知禮節

每來相對坐禪床

IN PRAISE
OF CH'AN MASTER WANG YOU
WHO CARES FOR THE BONNET MONKEYS
AROUND HIS MOUNTAIN STUDIO

From
Tree after tree
In the undisturbed courtyard
The fruit's dropped
On the frost.

They even love
Entering the thatched hall
To listen to *Dharma*. How is it
Other species know courtesy
And limits?

Coming in each time,
They sit opposite one another
On the meditation benches.

Chih Yuan

LOST CRANES

The pair
Of cranes suddenly
Flew off, their pure notes
Heard no more.

Perhaps
They're far away,
Obliged to seek immortal
Company, or close by, idly anxious
To avoid the chicken-flock. The lakebank
Quiet, water-watching's over, the courtyard
Empty, they've finished
The *Cloud Dance*.

All that's left
Are some old tracks
Like ancient writing, pressed
In the patterns
Of moss.

Chih Yuan

失鶴

隻鶴忽飛去清音更不聞遠應尋鳳侶閑恐避雞群

岸靜休臨水庭空罷舞雲唯餘舊蹤跡篆字印苔紋

Notes

Broken Tablets

▨ *Hsi Chou* was from Chien-nan, a T'ang administrative area extending from east of Kunming to west of Dali in Yunnan and north to about 200 kilometers north of Chengdu, comprising most of eastern and central Sichuan and northern Yunnan.

Sent to Huai Ku

▨ *T'iao-yin* probably refers to Mount T'iao-yin in Suide District, Shenxi Province. Present-day Suide District Town is at 110°20 E, 37°30 N. There is another mountain by this name about 200 kilometers southwest, near Lochuan District Town, at 109°30 E, 35°40 N.

▨ The *Ch'iang* people are tribes that lived, and still do live, in Gansu and northwest Sichuan.

▨ *Dawn piping* refers to the sound of a whistle, the *chia*, made from a reed. The *chia* was originally without holes for fingering, but these were later added. It is a traditional musical instrument of the Ch'iang people. Earlier travelers to the frontier, such as the late T'ang monk Wu K'e, noted this early-morning piping.

▨ *Our grove*, literally "beneath our woods," is a reference to Hsi Chou's monastery or hermitage and its precincts. Its derivation is similar to the word *academy*.

▨ *Zen*, Japanese for the Chinese *Ch'an*, has entered English as the name for that school of Buddhism which flourished in China as that country's original response to and vehicle for the teachings of Mahayana Buddhism.

Farewell to Wei Feng, Going to Far-South Mountain

▨ *Far-South Mountain (Chungnanshan*, about 40 kilometers SSE

of Xi'an, ancient Ch'ang-an, in south-central Shenxi Province)
is the principal mountain in a range of mountains that traverses
southern Shenxi, extending from the sacred Mount Song in
western Honan to the region of Tianshui in eastern Gansu. This
range is also called the *Ch'in-ling* or Ch'in Range.

- *The Pass* is the historic Hangu Pass, linking the north China
  plain with the region "inside the Pass," the old kingdom of
  Ch'in. It is located where the provinces of Shenxi, Honan, and
  Shanxi meet, just south of the great eastward bend of the Yellow
  River.

Early Spring at the Capital, Sent to the Honorable Kuan

- The *Honorable Kuan* was probably a Buddhist monk. The Sung
  capital was at Kaifeng in eastern Honan.
- The *Blue Gate* was the vernacular name for the southeastern
  gate in the city wall of the Han capital, Ch'ang-an, in south-
  central Shenxi. By the poets' time it had not existed for several
  hundred years, and is a reference to the capital and the political
  and social hurly-burly there that recluses and monks usually
  sought to avoid.

Autumn Path

- *Pao Hsien* was apparently from Chin-hua, a mountainous district in central Zhejiang Province called Jinhua. Present-day
  Jinhua District Town is at 119°30 E, 29°10 N.

Sent to Yuan Chen at White Cabin Peak

- *White Cabin Peak (Pai-ke Feng)* in Hu District, Shenxi, is part
  of the Chungnan or Ch'in Range of mountains. See "Farewell
  to Wei Feng Going to Far South Mountain." Present-day Hux-
  ian District Town is about 40 kilometers WSW of Xi'an.

Hearing the Gibbons Call in Pa Gorge

- The *gibbons*, a genus of small apes, the *hylobatidae*, range from
  Sumatra and the Malay peninsula to central China. They are

long-armed, tailless, have small naked callosities on the buttocks, and walk with their whole sole on the ground. They are considered the most agile of the old-world monkeys, and their unearthly cries have fascinated people and been the subject of poems for millennia.

The *Pa Gorges* of the Long River, near the border between Sichuan and Hubei, with their stunning cliffs and mountains are renowned for their scenic beauty and also as a haunt of the gibbons.

Wen Chao was from Nan-yueh, that is southern Zhejiang.

Farewell to Master Yu Chao

Hui-neng. Although scholars know very little about the late seventh-century monk, Hui-neng, Sixth Patriarch of the *Ch'an* (Jap. *Zen*) School of Chinese Buddhism, it would be impossible to overestimate his importance to the development of that school. The most revered account of his life, *The Platform Sutra of the Sixth Patriarch*, tells us that he was illiterate, as if to underscore his distance from intellectual understanding and closeness to the people. In one version, he attained enlightenment when he was selling firewood in the marketplace and heard a monk chanting from the *Diamond Sutra*. When the monk reached the passage where the Buddha says a bodhisattva "Should produce a thought that has nowhere to dwell," Hui- neng immediately understood its meaning.

It is from the time of Hui-neng that historians of Buddhism date the transformation of the Buddha's teachings from a foreign religion to a Chinese one. Since he spent most of his teaching ministry at Ts'ao-hsi Monastery in northern Guangdong, deep in South China, his teaching—asserting the immediate realization of the ultimate substance and purport of the buddha-mind—forms a basic part of what is called the Southern School of Chinese Buddhism.

Listening to Master Yu Chao Play the Lute

Traditionally, the *King Wen Rhythm* is a musical remonstrance (ts'ao) against the evils of the royal court of the moribund Shang dynasty (1766–1122 B.C.E.), composed by the posthumously titled King Wen of the succeeding Chou dynasty (1122–255 B.C.E.).

▓ The Master K'ung (552–478) founded the dominant school of Chinese philosophy called the *Ju*, the *Scholars*, or perhaps *Traditionalists*, which has produced the governors, historians, poets, statesmen, and the ethical and later speculative philosophers, whose achievements remain the major influence on Chinese society to the present time.

▓ Dusty heart, dusty mind, dusty thoughts, dusty world. The dust is always here, obscuring and irritating. It is the blinding dust of ignorance and of the defilements—greed, hatred, and delusion.

▓ Heng Chao was from Mount Tiantai in east-central Zhejiang Province. Present-day Tiantai District Town is at 121°E, 29° 10 N.

Farewell to Vinaya Master Ts'ung, Traveling in the West

▓ A *Vinaya master* was a member of the Buddhist order who made it his special duty to know and follow the many and complex rules for monks or nuns.

▓ The *Hangu Pass* is the major land route between Honan and Shenxi, the southern portion of which is the ancient kingdom of Ch'in.

▓ *Dusty eye.* People are always wanting to "open" Heavenly Eyes, Buddha Eyes, and so forth. This monk wants them to lose their dusty ones.

▓ Soon after Ts'ung-lu entered Ch'in through the Hangu Pass, he would approach the sacred mountain of the west, Mount Hua. On its east peak is a rock face called the Immortals Palm.

Given to Master Ch'ing-lun of Hsia Mountain

▓ *Hsia Mountain*, noted for its scenic beauty, is in the eastern part of Qing-yuan District, Guangdong Province. Present-day Qing-yuan District Town is about 75 kilometers NNW of

Guangzhou. There is a Buddhist monastery on the mountain and Taoists consider it the Nineteenth Place of Bliss (*Fu-ti*).

■ The *true rain* is the Dharma Rain. As the *P'u-men-p'in*, a chapter of the *Lotus Sutra* devoted to the worship of the Bodhisattva Avalokiteshvara, states, she "saturates with sweet dew and the Dharma rain, extinguishing the fires of the defilements."

■ Ye Creek is possibly Jo-ye Creek below Jo-ye Mountain near Shaoxing, Zhejiang, about 50 kilometers SE of Hangzhou.

■ Chien Chang was probably from Wo-chou Mountain in the eastern part of Xinchang District, Zhejiang Province. Xinchang District Town is at 120°50′ E, 29°30′ N.

Sent to Zen Master Yun-shui

■ Originally Bodhidharma's robe, the patriarch's robe, became a symbol of the orthodox transmission of the Dharma through successive generations of early patriarchs.

Staying with Master Heng Chao at Roost of the Sages Monastery on Mount Lu

■ Master Heng Chao was one of the Nine Monks. Roost of the Sages Monastery (*Hsi-hsien-ssu*), founded late in the fifth century, is located near the summit of Five Oldsters Peak (*Wu-lao Feng*), the southern eminence of Mount Lu. The peak is said to resemble five old men leaning on one another's shoulders. Mount Lu (29° 30′ N, 115° 55′ E), is in Jiangxi Province about 30 kilometers south of the city of Jiujiang. Surrounded by water on three sides, the mountain has been the residence of recluses from time immemorial and the site of many Buddhist establishments. Mist and fog frequently obscure its fantastic summits and cliffs, giving rise to the saying, "It's hard to see the true face of Mount Lu."

■ *The Greater Elegance*. The *Greater* and *Lesser Elegance* are two chapters of the *Classic of Poetry* (ca. 700–500 B.C.E.). The *Lesser Elegance* is concerned with food and drink, the reception of guests, important matters such as rewarding the labors of officials, attracting and maintaining wise and talented people, and even state and military policy. The *Greater Elegance* attends to the spiritual side of the monarchy, what might be called poems of the royal cult: its topics include receiving the mandate of Heaven to commence the Chou dynasty, attacking the Shang in order to replace them, assuming the prerogatives and revenues of the former kings, and honoring the ancestors in order to accord with Heaven. Thus the *Greater Elegance* praises the dynasty's very legitimacy. Master Wei Feng suggests that the sometimes slighted "poetry monks" can celebrate the spirit and accomplishments of Chinese Buddhism as the *Greater Elegance* celebrates the Royal Chou's. This would then constitute an even greater elegance.

By *method* Wei Feng is referring to what Buddhist sutras call the "skillful means," or methods, through which the Buddha and his followers reveal to people the truths of his teaching. Simile, metaphor, analogy, narrative skill, humor, pathos, and poetry, directed to the service of the Buddha's teaching, are all skillful means, as is the sensitivity to speak to each person and audience so that they become interested and comprehend in a profound sense. For Wei Feng, a "poetry monk" practices in the mainstream of the Buddha's teaching.

Heng-yang is a district in south-central Hunan. A portion of the slopes of Mount Heng, the southern sacred mountain, lies within the district boundaries. On one of Mount Heng's peaks is the well-known Chi-hsien, or Mount Heng Yueh, Monastery.

Wei Feng was from Mount Ch'ing-ch'eng in the area of present-day Guan District. Guan District Town is about 45 kilometers northwest of Chengdu, Sichuan.

Given to Wen Chao

King's Chamber Mountain (*Wang-wu Shan*) is a mountain in Yangcheng District, Shenxi Province (112°30 E, 35°25 N).

According to tradition the Yellow Emperor (ca. 2700 B.C.E.), who was a Taoist adept, sought the *Tao* on King's Chamber Mountain. This association must have drawn many recluses, and its relative proximity, about 190 kilometers WNW, to the Sung capital of Kaifeng apparently drew the attention of both Hui Ch'ung and his fellow monk Wen Chao. Yet the mountain's name itself is too suggestive to pass notice entirely: Is Hui Ch'ung examining his own motives for being in the capital, a milieu not usually esteemed by monks and hermits but ideal for furthering literary and artistic careers?

▨ Hui Ch'ung, a noted painter as well as a poet, was from Huai-nan, a Sung administrative area that extended inland along the Long River from the east coast to west of Hankou, Hubei Province, north from there to a point west of Xinyang, Honan Province, and northwest from there to the seacoast northwest of Huaiyin, Jiangsu Province.

The Pine Whisk

▨ *Deer-tail fly whisks*. Around the end of the Han dynasty and the first years of the Wei, that is, the first decades of the third century C.E., a kind of philosophical wit, the development of the Taoist traditions of Lao-tzu and Chuang-tzu, flourished in the highest governmental circles of the capital. These supramundane remarks and conversations were called *Pure Chat*, and in succeeding centuries it was within this tradition of Pure Chat that the literati of the Chinese upper class were first able to achieve a comprehensive understanding of the new teaching of the Buddha.

An emblem of the individual accomplished in the supernal wittiness of Pure Chat was a deer- or horse-tail whisk, sometimes called a fly-whisk, used to emphasize the speaker's ideas or attitudes. Out of poverty, frugality, and the wish to avoid animal products, recluses and Buddhist monks adapted a pine branch for their philosophical chats and lectures on Dharma.

▨ Though Yu Chao's *rocks in the woods* are not Tao Sheng's rocks on Tiger Mountain near Suzhou, it seems appropriate to tell their story here. One of the great achievements of the formative period of Chinese Buddhism was the translation of the sacred works of the Mahayana canon. Prominent lay intellectuals and poets aided monks from India and China in these efforts, and the growing Buddhist community in China eagerly awaited the translations that resulted from them. Besides the unfamiliar teachings each freshly translated Mahayana sutra introduced to the community, the newly available works were also used by Buddhists to resolve any doubtful points that might have already arisen among them about the Buddha's teaching. Indeed, some of these sacred works were translated more than once. In one case a difference between two versions of the *Mahaparinirvana Sutra* prolonged a critical misunderstanding about the buddha-nature itself.

Preached just before the Buddha's own nirvana, the *Mahaparinirvana Sutra* emphasizes the eternal, joyful aspects of nirvana and states that all sentient beings can attain buddhahood since they all possess the buddha-nature. Many Chinese Buddhists, familiar with the intimate yet impersonal emptiness of the wisdom sutras and the non-being of the Taoist classics, were at first diffident about these positive teachings. In fact, when the first translation of the *Mahaparinirvana Sutra* by Fa-hsien was made in 418 C.E., it stated that certain beings, called *icchantikas*, who have cut off their good roots, did not possess the buddha-nature and, hence, would never attain nirvana.

Some Buddhists did embrace the positive teachings of this final sutra of the Buddha's earthly life, and a certain monk, Tao Sheng (ca. 360–434), was enthusiastic about the eternal and joyous aspects of the newly translated work. Tao Sheng also became prominent for his insistence that the *icchantikas*, or those beings who had cut off their "good roots," which enable one to relate to the Buddha and his teaching, indeed did possess the buddha-nature and would ultimately attain nirvana. However most Buddhists, following the Fa-hsien translation of the sutra, believed the contrary. It was only more than a decade later when the more complete translation of Dharmakshema became available that the orthodoxy of Tao Sheng's view was validated, a view he had accepted through his understanding of buddha-nature, independent of—and indeed contrary to—accepted scriptural authority.

According to the *Record of the Monasteries of Wu*, during the period of his controversy Tao Sheng traveled to the south and later had a Lecture Hall on Tiger Hill outside of Suzhou. When he received the translation of Dharmakshema there, he set some stones upright as students and "broke off a pine branch to be his speaking whisk." He then preached the *Mahaparinirvana Sutra* before these listeners. When Tao Sheng reached the point where the sutra states: "The *icchantika* has the buddha-nature," he asked, "Does what I say accord with the buddha-mind?" Thereupon, the stones all bowed.

▓ Yu Chao was from Chiang-tung, a Sung administrative region that includes Anhui south of the Long River and the western tip of Jiangsu.

Living on the Plain in Early Autumn

▓ Huai Ku was from Mount O-mei, the sacred mountain in central Sichuan.

Living at a Monastery, Sent to Chien Chang

▓ Because "East Mountain" is something of a generic name, I am inclined to think it refers to a monastery on Wo-chou Mountain, though I have no evidence for this now.

▓ To *fly away on your walking stick* is a reference to the tradition that certain very advanced monks can fly with the aid of these staffs.

▓ Chien Chang was probably from Wo-chou Mountain in the eastern part of Xinchang District, Zhejiang Province. Xinchang District Town is at 120°50 E, 29°30 N.

Rotten Axe-Handle Mountain

▨ Rotten Axe-Handle Mountain (*Lan-ke Shan*) is in the southern part of Quxian, Zhejiang Province. Present-day Quxian District Town is at 118°55 E, 29°55 N. The mountain takes the name Lan-k'o, or *Rotten (Axe-) Handle*, from the tradition that it was the site of a *wei-ch'i* (Japanese: *go*) game between two Taoist immortals that lasted a hundred years. At the end of the game one of the players pointed out to Wang Chih, a wood-cutter who had wandered by and stopped to watch the game, that his axe-handle had rotted away.

▨ Stonebridge Mountain (*Shih-ch'iao shan*) is in Tiantai District of Zhejiang Province, some 250 kilometers northwest of Rotten Axe-Handle Mountain.

Living in Poverty

▨ For a brief account of Chih Yuan see the Introduction to this section.

In Praise of Ch'an Master Wang You Who Cares for the Bonnet Monkeys

▨ The Chinese bonnet monkey (*macacus sinicus*) is a heavily-built, dark-gray monkey with long hair radiating from a central point on the crown of the head and, like the gibbon, with naked callosities on the buttocks.

Lost Cranes

▨ The *Cloud Dance* is the name of an ancient dance. Pet cranes were frequently taught to dance.

Han-shan Te-ch'ing (1546–1623)

Translations by Red Pine

Introduction

I FIRST MET Han-shan Te-ch'ing in the spring of 1974. I was living in a Buddhist monastery in the hills south of Taipei, but every Saturday morning I left the sanctuary of Haiming Temple and followed a dirt trail through bamboo groves and past rice fields to the Shulin train station. I took the next local headed north and usually found room to stand in the baggage car. At least it was a quick trip: Panchiao, Wanhua, then Taipei. A few blocks from the Taipei station, I joined my future wife, Ku Lien-chang, at the Astoria Coffee Shop. We had met the previous year at the College of Chinese Culture, which I was attending between monasteries. She sat behind me in the class on Alfred North Whitehead, taught by Hsieh Yu-wei. Professor Hsieh had studied with Whitehead and Russell at Harvard, and I was still considering Western answers to the Buddhist view of reality.

After one semester, I decided I preferred monastic life, except on Saturdays. In addition to Whitehead, I also took a course on Lao-tzu's *Taoteching* and wanted to continue with the works of Chuang-tzu, Lao-tzu's successor in the Taoist pantheon. Ku suggested we begin with Han-shan Te-ch'ing's commentary to Chuang-tzu's text. And so I met Han-shan Te-ch'ing. Sometimes we were joined by the poet Dreaming Butterfly (Chou Meng-tieh), who sold poetry books from his sidewalk stall in front of the Astoria. And sometimes I brought along a bottle of cream sherry I kept at the monastery. Twenty-four years have passed since then, and Han-shan Te-ch'ing is once more with me, though Ku, Dreaming Butterfly, and the sherry are not. By way of introduction, I have added the following outline of Te-ch'ing's life to provide some background for the poems that follow.

Han-shan Te-ch'ing was born in 1546 near the Ming dynasty's southern capital of Nanking. At the age of twelve, he received his family's permission to enter Nanking's Paoen Monastery to fulfill his mother's vow to repay Kuan-yin, the Bodhisattva of Compassion, for saving him from a life-threatening illness during his infancy. The abbot gave the boy the name Te-ch'ing, meaning Purest Virtue. Purest Virtue studied with the Buddhist monks and Confucian teachers of Nanking until he was twenty-eight, at which point he put away his books and traveled north to the sacred mountain of Wutai. For eight years, he lived on Wutai's Han-shan Peak. And because he ascended the heights of the Dharma there, he added the peak's name to his own.

Wutai was also the scene of a special ceremony Te-ch'ing helped organize to ensure the birth of a male heir to the throne. When a boy was born to one of the emperor's concubines exactly nine months later, the emperor's mother became Te-ch'ing's lifelong supporter. Unfortunately, the emperor disagreed with his mother's choice of heir apparent, especially when a more favored concubine gave birth to a second son several years later.

Meanwhile, Te-ch'ing began writing the series of Buddhist works that were to make him one of the most revered monks in the realm, and he moved east to the Shantung coast. With the help of the emperor's mother, he built one of the largest Buddhist centers in all of China on Mount Laoshan overlooking the sea. But relations between the dowager and her son worsened as the issue of the heir split the loyalties of those at court, and Te-ch'ing was caught in the conflict. In 1595, he was arrested, defrocked, his new monastery burned to the ground, and he was sent into exile to the southernmost province of the empire.

Although at first he was required to report to the authorities, his fame as a Buddhist cleric eventually gained him the freedom to move about the region. In addition to organizing relief efforts during plagues and quelling a riot in the provincial capital of Canton, he also spent a number of years restoring the Buddhist center at Tsaohsi, 200 kilometers north of Canton. Tsaohsi was where Hui-neng, the Sixth Patriarch of Zen, transmitted the Dharma to the monks whose disciples founded the various Zen sects in China.

Finally, after nearly twenty years of exile, Te-ch'ing was pardoned and given his freedom in 1613. At first, he accepted the invitation of a fellow monk to spend his old age on Hengshan, Wutai's southern counterpart 300 kilometers north of Tsaohsi. Once more he shaved his head and donned his monk's robe. But after less than three years, he left Hengshan and traveled north to the Yangtze and then east to Nanking. Halfway to the southern capital, however, he stopped at Lushan and was sufficiently impressed with that mountain's scenery and serenity that he returned there in 1617 to spend his final years. But as his health declined, his disciples urged him to move back to Tsaohsi, and in 1622 he returned once more to Hui-neng's old temple in South China. He died the following year, and his body has been preserved there to this day along with that of Hui-neng, with whom he was linked by his disciples, who honored him as the Seventh Patriarch of Zen.

Since his death in the final years of the Ming, Te-ch'ing has been ranked as one of the most influential monks of one of China's greatest dynasties. Although he is best known for his commentaries on Buddhist, Taoist, and Confucian texts, as well as his philosophical essays, he was also a fine poet and composed the following verses shortly after he settled on Lushan and several years before his death. In their spare lines they reveal, far better than prose, the sensibility of someone at home with the Dharma as well as with the solitude of mountains and the unencumbered life of a monk.

Twenty-Eight Mountain Poems

ALL MY LIFE I have had a weakness for the wilderness and have traveled since my youth. When I was thirty, I lived for eight years among Wutai's ice and snow. I spent another twelve along the Eastern Sea. And when I was fifty, I was blown by the winds of karma to miasmic lands where I spent nearly twenty years. Our lives, alas, are brief. The years have come and gone, and suddenly I'm seventy. How long can a reflection or a shadow last? Recently, by the emperor's grace, I was allowed to resume my former life and proceeded to Hengshan to live out my old age. Conditions, however, were not ripe, and I came to this place in the East Lake region. With the help of several patrons, I began work on a hermitage on the full moon of the ninth month of Chia-yen (1617) and completed it shortly before the end of the twelfth month. It was all done very hastily. But now my heart has finally found a place to rest, like an old traveler who returns home and puts down his baggage and finally enjoys peace and leisure. What could be more delightful?

Whenever I speak in public, attendants record my words. But to express my deeper thoughts, I turn to unspoken verse. I have written down the following poems as the mood arose and without any order in mind.

祇園借得一枝安
從此無論道路難
日上三竿高臥穩
相看不必勸加餐

In Jetavana Park I found a place to rest
no more do I discuss the trials of the road
when the sun is three hands high I'm still sound asleep
no need at receptions to urge me to eat more

雪壓衡門夜擁爐
此身雖寄恰如無
不知日月從何去
回首人間歲已徂

Snow besieges my plank door I crowd the stove at night
although this form exists it seems as if it doesn't
I have no idea where the months have gone
every time I turn around another year on earth is over

A tiny hut in a world of plants
a bed of stone a thatched-roof shrine
a closed doorway like Vimilakirti's
don't ask about the bunch in front or back

My body is like deadwood my thoughts are like ashes
there's snow on my skull and frost on my jaw
I don't disdain the world just because I'm old
dust finds no place to land in my eyes

灌木叢中一小菴 石床爲座草爲籠
杜門口似維摩詰 莫問前三與後三

形如枯木念如灰 雪滿頭顱霜滿腮
不是老來偏厭世 眼中無處著塵埃

身心放下有餘閒　垂老生涯在萬山
不許白雲輕出谷　好隨明月護柴關

I let mind and body go and gained a life of freedom
my old age is taking place among ten thousand peaks
I don't let white clouds leave the valley lightly
I escort the moon as far as my closed gate

寒燈獨照影微微　疏屋風吹雪滿衣
忽憶五臺趺坐處　萬年冰裏一柴扉

A solitary winter lantern casts a feeble shadow
wind blows through my flimsy hut and covers me with snow
I remember sitting cross-legged on Wutai
a makeshift door amid ten-thousand-year-old ice

Bone-chilling snow on a thousand peaks
wild raging wind from ten thousand hollows
when I first awake deep beneath my blanket
I forget my body is in a silent void

A hundred thousand worlds are flowers in the sky
a single mind and body is moonlight on the water
once the cunning ends and information stops
at that moment there is no place for thought

寒威入骨千峰雪　怒氣衝人萬竅風
衲被蒙頭初睡醒　不知身在寂寥中

百千世界空華影　一片身心水月光
伎倆窮時消息斷　可中無處著思量

地爐無火石床寒
瓦鼎香消坐夜殘
萬籟聲沉心更寂
卻疑身在鏡中看

The fire pit is cold the stone bed like ice
the clay censer died before the end of night
the world of sound is silent my mind completely still
and now it seems my body exists inside a mirror

四圍嘉樹影扶疏
樹下深藏一小廬
車馬不聞人跡斷
閉門長日獨跏趺

The shade of noble trees spreads in all directions
below the trees a tiny hut is perfectly secluded
beyond the sound of cart or horse or sign of human tracks
all day behind my door I sit alone cross-legged

A hard cold rain a forest of wind
late at night the lotus drips
who knows the dream that entrances the world
is simply the luminous *prajna* mind

寒雨瀟瀟風滿林
蓮花漏永夜沉沉
誰知舉世難醒夢
盡是光明般若心

Late at night I sit alone and work on deadwood zen
I stir the lifeless ashes the fire won't relight
suddenly I hear the tower chime resound
its single sound of clarity fills the winter sky

夜深獨坐事枯禪
撥盡寒灰火不然
忽聽樓頭鐘磬發
一聲清韻滿霜天

雪滿乾坤萬象新　白銀世界裏藏身
坐來頓入光明藏　此處從來絕點塵

Snow covers earth and sky everything is new
my body is concealed inside a silver world
suddenly I enter a treasury of light
a place forever free of any trace of dust

平湖冷浸荇荷衣　湖上青山絕是非
塵跡盡消人世遠　白雲鷗鳥總忘機

Flat Lake cold penetrates water-lily clothes
the mountain by the lake is neither right nor wrong
dusty tracks all end the world is far away
white clouds and gulls have no hidden plans

Snow obstructs my brushwood door with me inside alone
one by one coral branches break in winter woods
in the light of dawn mountain green is gone
if the plums have finished blooming I for one can't tell

Spring has come again the snow has finally stopped
the crescent moon and leafless trees look thinner than before
at night I push my window open and gaze into space
beyond my pillared eaves spreads a sky of stars

雪擁柴扉獨坐時
寒林寸寸折瓊枝
曉來頓失青山色
開盡梅花總不知

春過人日雪初晴
新月疏林影更清
夜起推窗望寥廓
滿天星斗挂簷楹

雲開四野動春光　何處梅花送暗香
曳杖欲尋幽谷去　一枝斜倚在東墻

Clouds release the hillsides and wake the scenes of spring
where is the plum tree that wafts that subtle scent
I grab my staff intending to search secluded valleys
then find a single branch against my eastern wall

一片雲封萬壑松　門前流水日淙淙
不分晝夜供鼾睡　好夢驚回隔嶺鐘

A single cloud envelops ten-thousand streamside pines
before my door the flowing water babbles all the time
no matter if it's day or if it's night I snore
until the bell across the ridge ends my blissful dreams

After late spring rain the falling petals swirl
weightlessly celestial scent covers my patched robe
a simple vacant mind has no place to go
resting on the peak I watch the clouds return

春深雨過落花飛
冉冉天香上衲衣
一片閒心無處著
峰頭倚杖看雲歸

I follow my impulsive feet wherever they might go
my body is a pine tree surrounded by the snow
sometimes I simply stand beside a flowing stream
sometimes I chase a drifting cloud past another peak

信步騰騰任所從
形骸一似雪中松
偶來纔向溪頭立
又逐閒雲過別峰

麋鹿空山孰可從
輸他豐草與長松
紅塵縱有難醒夢
絕世何曾到萬峰

Who can be a wild deer among deserted mountains
satisfied with tall grass and pines
if the realm of dust was an endless dream
how then did heroes reach the land of peaks

垂垂白髮對青山
身在千巖萬壑間
寂寂松門無過客
往來唯有白雲閒

My long white hair is framed by green mountains
my body is surrounded by a thousand cliffs and gorges
the pine gate is silent no one passes by
the only ones who visit are the drifting clouds

The mountains stand unmoving just the way they are
all day they let the clouds roll out and roll back in
even though red dust is countless layers deep
not a single speck reaches my thatched hut

Deep among ten thousand peaks I sit alone cross-legged
a solitary thought fills my empty mind
my body is the moon that lights the winter sky
in rivers and in lakes are only its reflections

青山不動自如如　朝暮雲霞任卷舒
縱有紅塵深萬丈　曾無一點到茅廬

萬峰深處獨跏趺　歷歷虛明一念孤
身似寒空挂明月　唯餘清影落江湖

129

睡起呼童旋煮茶
竹爐湯沸雪如花
旗鎗未豎魔先退
始信叢林有作家

I wake up a novice and ask him to make tea
as the bamboo tea stove glows snow turns into flowers
before the spear and flag are raised Mara disappears
finally admitting the temple has a master

倦倚虛窗坐看山
千峰紫翠出松間
無心縱許雲來往
何似如如體更閒

Resting at my open window I gaze out at mountains
a thousand peaks of blue and purple rise above the pines
without a thought or care white clouds come and go
so utterly accepting so totally relaxed

Moonlight and the sound of pines are things we all know
zen mind and delusion distinguish sage and fool
go back to the place where not one thought appears
how shall I put this into words for you

月色松聲總見聞　禪心妄想聖凡分
消歸一念無生處　此意如何把似君

Flat Lake's autumn water merges with the winter sky
the ancient trees are limned with frost the falling leaves are red
the stone path and the footbridge are free of human tracks
a single hut is locked away deep inside the clouds

平湖秋水浸寒空　古木霜飛落葉紅
石徑小橋人跡斷　一菴深鎖白雲中

Notes

1. In Jetavana Park I found a place to rest

Jetavana was the name of a private park outside the ancient Indian city of Shravasti (near modern Balrampur). It was purchased from Prince Jeta by the Buddha's lay supporters for the Order's use during its summer retreat. It was also the scene of the Buddha's *Diamond Sutra*, in which he tells Subhuti to practice without letting his mind rest anywhere (10). In this poem, the sanctuary of Lushan's Wujih Peak takes Jetavana's place, as it was purchased for use as Te-ch'ing's retreat. Three hands is the period between eight and nine o'clock. Receptions include the ordinary social variety but also those at which Zen masters meet with disciples or visitors for the purpose of spiritual instruction. The last couplet recalls Wang Wei's *Drinking Wine with P'ei Ti*: "The world's passing clouds aren't worth our time / and not like sleeping soundly or having more to eat." To which Lao-tzu would have added: "thus the rule of the sage / empties the mind / but fills the stomach" (*Taoteching*: 3).

2. Snow besieges my plank door I crowd the stove at night

"Plank door" is literary shorthand for the home of someone who has retired from active involvement in government service or politics into anonymity. Buddhists view our existence on Earth as humans as but one of a series of stops on the Wheel of Karma.

3. A tiny hut in a world of plants

The stone bed, which also appears in verse 9, most likely refers to a hard bed—although for some hermits it was, in fact, a stone bed. The closed doorway also refers to the mouth and among Buddhists indicates the inexpressible Dharma. In his *Wuming-lun*, Seng-chao noted, "Shakyamuni shut his hut in Magadha.

Vimilakirti closed his doorway in Vaishali." Vimilakirti was a Buddhist layman who assumed the guise of poverty and illness to elicit a visit from the Buddha's disciples. But because he had previously exposed their limited understanding of the Dharma, only Manjushri, the Bodhisattva of Wisdom, dared convey the Buddha's greetings. The last line refers to Wu-chu's (820–899) encounter with an incarnation of Manjushri. While visiting Mount Wutai, Wu-chu met an old monk who led him inside a temple and asked him how monks practiced the Dharma in Hangchou. Wu-chu said, "In this Dharma-ending age most monks just follow the precepts." The old monk asked, "How many monks live there?" Wu-chu answered, "Three or four hundred." Then Wu-chu asked, "How is the Dharma practiced here?" The old monk said, "The dragons and snakes are hard to tell apart. Sages and fools all live here together." Wu-chu asked, "And how many are there?" The old monk replied, "There's a bunch in front and a bunch in back." Then he shouted "Hey!" and offered Wu-chu tea and cakes. Pointing to a crystal cup, he asked, "Do you have these in the south?" Wu-chu said, "No." The old monk continued, "And what do you drink tea with?" Wu-chu didn't know what to say and got up to leave. The old monk asked a novice to see Wu-chu to the gate. As he was leaving, Wu-chu asked the novice, "How many are there in the bunch in front and the bunch in back?" The novice shouted, "Great Monk!" Wu-chu said, "Yes?" The novice said, "That's how many." Wu-chu asked, "What's the name of this place?" The novice said, "The Diamond Cave of Wisdom." Suddenly Wu-chu realized the old monk was Manjushri (*Wutenghuiyuan*: 20).

4. *My body is like deadwood my thoughts are like ashes*
"Deadwood" is short for "deadwood zen" and refers to the effects of prolonged meditation. In Te-ch'ing's case, his legs became so crippled from lack of circulation that he required assistance to walk any distance. Dust refers to the Buddhist view of sensation as illusion.

5. *I let mind and body go and gained a life of freedom*
"Mind and body" is shorthand for the five *skandhas* that make up what passes for the individual, with form comprising the body and sensation, perception, impulse, and consciousness comprising the mind. White clouds also refer to wandering monks.

6. *A solitary winter lantern casts a feeble shadow*
A "winter lantern" refers to a lantern with the barest of wicks. Such lanterns were used at temples and wayside inns to help residents and visitors find their way about during the long winter nights. Here, the "winter lantern" also refers to the moon. The five peaks after which Wutaishan is named are located 250 kilometers southwest of Beijing and are the sacred residence of Manjushri, the Bodhisattva of Wisdom. The mountain is also known for its long, cold winters as well as its solitude. This was where Te-ch'ing experienced enlightenment and where he wrote his first essays on the Dharma. This was also where his practice of prolonged meditation in extreme cold led to severe rheumatism in his knees.

7. *Bone-chilling snow on a thousand peaks*
The image and wording of the second line is indebted to *Chuangtzu*: 2.1, where Chuang-tzu traces the origin of wind to hollows in the earth and likens these to our sense organs.

8. *A hundred thousand worlds are flowers in the sky*
As in verse 5, "mind and body" refers to the individual as made up of parts that come together temporarily and which include no permanent self. I am indebted to Ting Fu-pao's *Dictionary of Buddhist Terms* (p. 832) for my reading of *k'o-chung: at that moment.*

9. *The fire pit is cold the stone bed like ice*
The image in a mirror is one of ten similes used in the *Prajnaparamita Sutra* to explain the illusory nature of phenomena.

10.   *The shade of noble trees spreads in all directions*
The third line recalls the opening lines of one of T'ao Yuan-ming's *Drinking Poems*: "I built my hut beside a path / but hear no sound of cart or horse" (5). T'ao's fifth-century hut was only three kilometers southeast of Te-ch'ing's seventeenth-century retreat. To sit cross-legged is to meditate in what is also called the "lotus position."

11.   *A hard cold rain a forest of wind*
Here the lotus, symbol of liberation from the muddy waters of delusion and suffering, takes the form of a water clock used to measure periods of meditation. *Prajna* is the Sanskrit word for wisdom. The last couplet recalls Hui-neng's exposition of *prajna* insight: "Mortals are buddhas. Delusion is enlightenment" (*Sutra of the Sixth Patriarch*: 2).

12. *Late at night I sit alone and work on deadwood zen*
"Deadwood zen" refers to the practice of prolonged meditation. The temple bell is used to mark periods in the monastic round, which begins in many monasteries around 4 A.M. with an hour of meditation.

13. *Snow covers earth and sky everything is new*
Ch'ien-k'un: earth and sky are the first two hexagrams in the *I-ching: Book of Changes* and represent the opposite and complementary forces of yin and yang and, thus, of creation. The mention of dust recalls Hui-neng's famous poetic response to Shen-hsiu's poem. Shen-hsiu wrote: "The body is the Bodhi tree / the mind is like a perfect mirror / always keep it clean / don't let it gather dust." Hui-neng replied: "Bodhi is no tree / what's perfect is no mirror / actually there isn't a thing / where do you get this dust?"

14. *Flat Lake cold penetrates water-lily clothes*
Pinghu: Flat Lake must be another name for Poyanghu, China's

largest freshwater lake over 5,000 square kilometers in area. Te-ch'ing's hut was five kilometers northwest of the northwest corner of the lake. Hermits did on rare occasions patch their clothes with lotus and water-lily pads in summer, though not for long, as both soon become brittle. Still, they represented the imagined attire of the blameless recluse. Here, however, they fail to withstand the reality of Lushan's winter weather. The last line recalls the following story from *Liehtzu*: "There once was a young man who lived by the sea and loved seagulls. Whenever he walked along the shore, more than a hundred birds would follow him. One day his father told him to catch a few and bring them back to keep as pets. The next day, when the young man went walking along the shore, not one gull would approach him" (2.11). Here the gulls would be from Poyang Lake, and the white clouds would also refer to wandering monks. A poem by the T'ang hermit Ssu K'ung-t'u includes the line, "When words include no hidden plans, buddhahood is near."

15. Snow obstructs my brushwood door with me inside alone

A "coral branch" is a euphemism for an imperial heir, and the *han-lin: winter woods* is a homophone for the Hanlin Academy of scholars that advised the emperor. This would seem to be an instance of *lèse majesté*, as Te-ch'ing was exiled for his involvement in supporting the "wrong" heir to the throne and thus opposing the choice of the emperor and his advisors. As it turned out, both sons died before they could assume the throne. Here, the coral branches also refer to leafless limbs breaking under the weight of fresh snow.

16. Spring has come again the snow has finally stopped

In China, spring begins with the first moon of the new year. The use of extended eaves supported by posts or pillars is common along the perimeter of monastery shrine halls. It is also common in areas of heavy rainfall. Currently Lushan reports an average of 1,917 millimeters, or 76 inches, of rainfall per year, which exceeds all but the rainiest rain forests of the contiguous United States. Thus, the mountain is famous for its waterfalls, its mist, and its constantly changing views.

17. *Clouds release the hillsides and wake the scenes of spring*
Looking for the first plum blossoms remains a rite of spring in China, especially among poets.

18. *A single cloud envelops ten-thousand streamside pines*
The bell could be that of any number of temples. Within a two-kilometer radius of Te-ch'ing's hut (and the adjacent hermitage of Fayun Temple) were Huangyen Temple, Kaihsien Temple, Hsiufeng Temple, and Wanshan (Ten Thousand Firs) Temple, the last of which is mirrored by the pines in the first line. Kueit-sung Temple, Lushan's earliest and largest monastic complex, was about five kilometers to the south.

19. *After late spring rain the falling petals swirl*
Monks originally sewed their robes from patches of discarded clothing. By Te-ch'ing's time, however, such robes were usually made of a specific number of pieces of new material sewn together to represent various numerical aspects of Buddhist teaching. In the *Vimilakirti Sutra*, flowers falling from the sky are unable to cling to the robes of Vimilakirti or the assembled bodhisattvas, whereas the lesser disciples in attendance are unable to shake them off because of their attachment to form (7).

20. *I follow my impulsive feet wherever they might go*
The stark image of the pine tree in winter reminds us that Te-ch'ing's legs were crippled. Thus, his "impulsive feet" should be understood as referring to the wanderings of his spirit. The phrase *hsueh-chung-sung: pine tree in the snow* was also a metaphor for unchanging virtue amid difficult times.

21. *Who can be a wild deer among deserted mountains*
Hermits were often referred to as "wild deer" (as opposed to the deer kept in enclosures for the amusement of the wealthy). Red dust refers to the illusory glory of fame and power, as well as to sensation in general.

22. *My long white hair is framed by green mountains*
Although monks and nuns shave their heads twice a month, elderly hermits often exempt themselves from such monastic decorum. The pine gate refers to the pairs of evergreens planted on either side of a monastery entrance and, by extension, to the monastery itself. Here, it probably refers to the modest halls of Fayun Temple, which was built (in three and a half months, according to Te-ch'ing's preface) near Te-ch'ing's hut to accommodate his disciples and occasional visitors. Clouds also refer to wandering monks.

23. *The mountains stand unmoving just the way they are*
As with the flowers in verse 19, the red dust of illusion only settles on those who remain convinced that it is real and worthy of consideration. The color red is the color of heat, life, and attraction.

24. *Deep among ten thousand peaks I sit alone cross-legged*
The body in line 3 is our buddha-nature. The expression "rivers and lakes" refers to the lower reaches of the Yangtze and includes the Hsiang River/Tung-ting Lake watershed, the Kan River/Poyang Lake watershed, and the Taihu Lake watershed. This was the region where Zen developed from the seeds planted by Bodhidharma into the spiritual tradition now practiced around the world. Thus, the expression also refers to the life of wandering and seclusion that was characteristic of its early practitioners.

25. *I wake up a novice and ask him to make tea*
Senior monks were usually accompanied by an attendant, especially when they had as much trouble walking as Te-ch'ing did.

It was Te-ch'ing's practice to meditate through the night. To stay awake monks relied on tea. The "poor-man's" stove used here for heating water consisted of a single section of large-diameter bamboo with an opening at the base for coals and whose top rim supported the teapot. Some tea masters did use snow to make tea, but most connoisseurs preferred the water of a mountain spring. The spear and flag refer to the unopened bud and single adjacent leaf of the tea plant, whose tips were harvested in this fashion several times a year to produce the finest tea. Mara is the king of all demons who work to distract those who seek enlightenment.

26. *Resting at my open window I gaze out at mountains*
As elsewhere, clouds also refer to wandering monks.

27. *Moonlight and the sound of pines are things we all know*
The word *zen:ch'an* is the transliteration in Japanese and Chinese respectively of the Sanskrit *dhyana*, which refers to meditation or trance. Odd as it may seem, the Japanese pronunciation has preserved that of China's T'ang dynasty, while China's Mandarin dialect has not. In any case, not long after Bodhidharma arrived in China, the word was extended to include the practices developed by his disciples to direct people to their original, undifferentiated minds, regardless of whether or not formal meditation was involved. Although the distinction is sometimes difficult to make, I usually capitalize the word where it refers to the lineage of teachers and leave it in small case where it refers to meditation and its state of trance, as well as the techniques used by Zen masters to free practitioners from the attachment to trance.

28. *Flat Lake's autumn water merges with the winter sky*
When the travel diarist Hsu Hsiao-k'o visited the southern slopes of Lushan in 1618, the year after Te-ch'ing settled there, he reported seeing a very neat and picturesque hut below Yellowstone Cliff surrounded by tall bamboos, maple trees, and

myriad flowers. Was this Te-ch'ing's hut or that of a fellow hermit? In any case, Hsu noted that Poyang Lake was visible from there and made no mention of any other lake. Hence, I assume, as in verse 14, that *Pinghu: Flat Lake* was another name for Poyanghu.

Bibliography

SOURCE FOR THE POEMS

Han-shan lao-jen meng-yu-chi (The Dream Journeys of Old Man Han-shan). Vol. 49. Hong Kong: Hong Kong Buddhist Book Distributors, 1965.

ENGLISH TRANSLATIONS OF WORKS BY HAN-SHAN TE-CH'ING

Cryer, James M. "Mountain Living: Twenty Poems." In *A Drifting Boat: An Anthology of Chinese Zen Poetry*, edited by J.P. Seaton and Dennis Maloney. Fredonia, NY: White Pine Press, 1994.

Lu, K'uan-yu (Charles Luk). *Ch'an and Zen Teaching*. 3 vols. London: Rider, 1960–62.

_____. *The Secrets of Chinese Meditation: Self-cultivation by Mind Control as Taught in the Ch'an, Mahayana, and Taoist Schools in China*. London: Rider, 1964.

_____. *The Surangama Sutra, with an Abridged Commentary by Ch'an Master Han-shan Te-ch'ing*. London: Rider, 1966.

_____. *Practical Buddhism*. London: Rider, 1971.

Sheng-yen. *Getting the Buddha Mind*. Elmhurst, NY: Dharma Drum Publications, 1982.

ENGLISH STUDIES OF HAN-SHAN TE-CH'ING

Pei-yi, Wu. "The Spiritual Autobiography of Te-ch'ing." In *The Unfolding of Neo-Confucianism*, edited by Wm. Theodore de Bary. New York: Columbia University Press, 1975.

Sung-peng, Hsu. *A Buddhist Leader in Ming China: The Life and Thought of Han-shan Te-ch'ing*. University Park: Pennsylvania State University Press, 1979.

石
樹

From Stones and Trees:
The Poetry of Shih-shu
(late 17th century–early 18th century)

Translations by
James H. Sanford

INTRODUCTION

WE REALLY DON'T KNOW who Shih-shu was. The name Shih-shu appears to be a pseudonym used one time only for the poet's contributions to a single text, known in modern times as the *T'ien-t'ai san sheng erh ho shih chi* (*Anthology of the Poems of the Three Sages of T'ien-t'ai and Their Two Harmonizers*). This text consists of three layers. The first of these is an edition of the collected works of the well-known Zen madman and poet Han-shan, who flourished around 650 C.E. Alone, this layer constitutes the *Han-shan shih chi* (*Poems of Cold Mountain*). But, in fact, both the standard *Han-shan shih chi* and the harmonized *T'ien-t'ai san sheng erh ho shih chi* version (hereafter, the *Three Sages Harmonies*) contain not only the 307 poems attributed to Han-shan. They also contain forty-nine poems attributed to his co-conspirator in Buddhist mischief and weird poetry, Shih-te, and two poems attributed to their somewhat reclusive fellow traveler, the Zen monk Feng-kan (perhaps best known for his habit of using a pet tiger as a naptime pillow). Together, these three are the Three Sages of Mount T'ien-t'ai.

To the basic Han-shan anthology of 358 original poems, the *Three Sages Harmonies* adds a second layer consisting of "harmony poems" by Ch'u-shih Fan-ch'i (1296–1370). A harmony poem is a poem that is written in the same structural format and meter as an admired original poem and which at key word positions is also required to use the very same Chinese character as the original. Harmony poems thus constitute a sort of "poems in the style of" genre. Since Ch'u-shih was a major Buddhist figure in his century—as well as a prolific poet—his harmonies are a clear indication that by his day Han-shan and Shih-te, in spite of the ragged, colloquial style of their poetry, had become mainstream literary figures worthy of admiration and imitation.

The third layer of the *Three Sages Harmonies* text, the one which concerns us most directly here, is a further set of harmonies— harmonies to Han-shan, Shih-te, and Feng-kan, but to Ch'u-shih's earlier harmonies to the Three Sages as well. These are the harmony poems produced by Shih-shu. Shih-shu literally means "stones and trees." According to legend, stones and trees—not paper and silk— were the first venue of the Han-shan and Shih-te poems in the T'ang dynasty. The name Shih-shu is thus a transparent evocation of this legend, and almost certainly a single-usage pen name.

What we can actually know of Shih-shu has only two sources: the content and style of his harmonies in the *Three Sages Harmonies* and what little he tells us in his brief headnote to these poems. This headnote or preface is dated 1703, and its signature line tells us that it was "written at Stone-sprout Peak on the Yellow Sea by the follower of the Way Shih-shu, who is also know as T'ung-yin." In his note, Shih-shu tells us that years earlier he had encountered a copy of the Han-shan (Shih-te, and Feng-kan) Collection with Chu-shih's harmonies appended to it. Of this encounter he says, "When I first read his work, I did not know that the Three Sages were Ch'u-shih and Ch'u-shih the Three Sages. But on rereading him it was as if the Three Sages were right there in front of me—such is the unique quality of his work. Thereafter, whenever and wherever I encountered beautiful mountains or imposing waters, felt a gentle wind, or saw the clear moon, I could not help but chant out these brief songs." For two decades Shih-shu hesitated to dare harmonies of his own to these illustrious poems, but at last he took up "…the rhymes of the three poets and made [my] own rock and tree (*shih-shu*) poems." In less than a month he managed to finish them all. At the end of his preface, still uncertain if his renderings have equaled "the understanding and compassion" of his forerunners, Shih-shu says he will "…for now tuck [my] poems away, out of sight, on this celebrated mountain. Perhaps after another five hundred years someone will come along, read them, and add harmonies of his own."

Shih-shu's harmonies were not, of course, intended as autobiography. The reader is free to make what he or she will of the poems and of their author as well. Still, a few suggestions may be in order. Unlike the earlier harmonizer, Ch'u-shih, Shih-shu is not a very insistent Buddhist. While Ch'u-shih tows a fairly orthodox line, Shih-shu—typical of his era perhaps—seems as much Taoist as Buddhist, more a lay hermit than an entempled monk. Indeed, many of his poems use images and vocabulary derived entirely from the Taoist alchemical tradition. Further, as a Buddhist, he is clearly of the "samsara is itself nirvana" variety; for him, the world is far more a realm of enlightenment than a prison-house of sorrow. Indeed, at times he even seems to approach the tantric view of esoteric Buddhism and its watchword "the passions are themselves enlightenment."

Accordingly, major themes in Shih-shu are a closeness to nature, spiritual transformation within the world, and a glorification of the hermit life of solitude and poverty. But whether in the end these themes reflect Shih-shu's own life and times or are, instead, only spiritual or poetic ideals is a question we cannot answer anymore than we can say who Shih-shu himself *really* was.

Finally, I might note that as a poet Shih-shu stands well above Ch'u-shih and often surpasses Feng-kan, Shih-te, and Han-shan as well. He need not have worried himself about having to tuck his own poems out of sight somewhere by the Yellow Sea. They are much better off out in the open—where anybody can read and appreciate them.

All but three of the Shih-shu harmonies translated here trace back to Han-shan originals. To compare a Shih-shu harmony to its original model—in English rendering at least—one may look up the same-numbered poem in Red Pine's translation of Han-shan (*The Collected Songs of Cold Mountain*, Copper Canyon Press, 1983). The three unnumbered poems are harmonies to Shih-te.

35

the solitary peak stands alone—high, aloof
its shallow brooks frozen, still
overhead dancing clouds soar and wheel: a flock of birds
and jumbled boulders seem, men in conversation

its bones, pale white plum blossoms
its flesh, luxuriant green sedges
softly, distantly; song from another world
every verse a harmony on the warmth of spring

崒崒高峰頂冷冷淺水濱飄飄雲似鳥磊磊石如人白
白梅花骨青青蒲葉身悠悠世外曲句句和陽春

人富愁貧日吾貧如富年萬峰隨分住不用一文錢澗

水茅簷下巖花竹檻前寒來可曝背暑氣坐涯邊

40

the rich worry about getting poor
for me poverty would be a good year
I followed fate into these myriad peaks
you don't need a penny here

thatched eaves beside a racing brook
cragflowers draping the bamboo fence
in winter, I turn my back to the sun
come summer, park myself at water's edge

against the gently flowing spring morning
the arrogant rattle of a passing coach
peach blossoms beckon from the distant village
willow branches caress the shoulder of my pond

as bream and carp flash their golden scales
and mated ducks link embroidered wings
the poet stares about; this way, then that—
caught in a web beyond all speaking

春日正遲遲遊車驕自許桃花迎遠村楊柳拂清渚魴
鯉躍金鱗鴛鴦交錦羽詩人縱曠觀安得竟無語

有日空之宗無乃數之極毫末成花種普天歸帝力禽
魚自飛躍男女安衣食奇哉造化工一氣吞五色

some speak of ancestral emptiness
a nothing that is yet an infinity
smallest hint of a germ of a blossom
yet, the whole world subject to its call

fish swim and animals leap with it
men and women are fed and clothed by it
strange, indeed, its transmutations
one breath swallowing up five colors

不負梅花約而來住庵蓬窗蒼霰入紙被雪花氅厓
倒寒冰樹雲深冷石潭此時燒榾柮吾道在江南

rather than break my vow to plum blossoms
I have settled here in this disheveled hut
grey sleet seeps through briars at my window
plumes of snow dance around its papered panes

steep scarps loom above frozen woods
deep clouds conceal the pool's icy stones
such weather; I stoke up a few charcoal twigs
wish for a way south—to Chiang-nan's shore

叮嚀學道人無事勿相失花間襯綠雲松頭落紅日春
深鳥語頻秋老蟲聲唧曉了此中玄可云參學畢

a charge to students of the Tao:
"nothing to do; nothing to lose"
among the flowers, darkening clouds
above the pines, a sinking sun

spring deepens with urgent birdcalls
autumn declines to the cries of insects
dawn: darkness wrapped in darkness
this, the end of every quest

93

you can't negate negation
so how can being be?
yesterday I saw a young fellow on a horse
leading a bride home to his garden

for a few years they looked like flowers
but with age turned ugly, wrinkled
bound together, but not by rope
shuffling their feet, first one, then the other

無之不可無有者如何有昨見馬上郎娶歸園中婦初
年貌如花老去顏多醜緊縛不是繩步步隨他走

學道莫乾苦疑情須發真掃開千件事拌此一生身秋
去黃花盡春來綠葉新靜中觀物理何者可愁人

37

study the Way and never grow old
distrust emotions; truth will emerge
sweep away your worries
set even your body aside

autumn drives off the yellow leaves
yet spring renews every green bud
quietly contemplate the pattern of things
nothing here to make us sad

70

as flowing waters disappear into the mist
we lose all track of their passage
every heart is its own Buddha
ease off; become immortal

wake up: the world's a mote of dust
behold heaven's round mirror
turn loose: slip past shape and shadow
sit side by side with nothing—save Tao

流水行雲處因之見不遷有心皆作佛無事即爲仙悟
世微塵窄窺天一鏡圓頹然形影外惟與道相連

夢中偶看月五采霞光織織女下階來不借雲之力問
我是何名我答云不識松風忽吹來紅日映窗色

137

in a dream I see the moon
beams of light woven all around it
the Weaver Girl descends step by step
not even a cloud to hold her up

she asks my name
"No one you'd know," I reply
suddenly a pine breeze swirls by
dazzling sunbeams flood my window

nonsense: these Buddha teachings
illuminating moving bowels and passing water
ignorant of the wellspring of spirituality
they pour mountains and oceans from the same hole

fur and hair are easily tangled
as the Black Wind whistles its ghastly tune
yet, heed not the howling jackals' cry
rather, relieve yourself among the singing frogs

謬說佛法者分明運屎尿不知宗教源山海同其竅毛
髮有差訛黑風吹鬼調不為野干鳴便作蝦蟆叫

人方寸施肝膽萬里見苟不本所從茫茫梁上燕
人身小天地寒涕如飛霰皮裏載溪山胸中藏郡縣智

the human body is a little universe
its chill tears, so much wind-blown sleet
beneath our skins, mountains bulge, brooks flow
within our chests lurk lost cities, hidden tribes

wisdom quarters itself in our tiny hearts
liver and gall peer out, scrutinize a thousand miles
follow the path back to its source, else be
a house vacant save for swallows in the eaves

others know how to forge metals
meld them back into a singularity
they push aside "the man of no position"
slap the silly Zennists down

disputing the tiger; disputing the dragon
calling out the ox; calling out the horse
what kind of place is this anyway?
which has no high—has no low

別有煆鍊才總歸一大冶推出無位人打徹癡禪者辯
虎兼辯龍呼牛復呼馬此間是何境擬議非高下

虛空大文章函蓋乾坤部點墨化雙龍看雲變蒼狗缽
底山河藏胸中日月走猛風吹古嵐草木知哮吼

emptiness is a long story
that swallows up heaven and earth
a splash of ink turns into two dragons
stray clouds become an azure dog

lurking in my bowl: mountains, rivers
wheeling through my breast: a sun, a moon
a fierce wind shreds the ancient mists
grasses and trees bow before its snap and snarl

69

mountains and rivers: flowers of the Tao
but I, sadly, am a writer
no divine voice, talentless
yet, lend me a brush; I'm off and running

better an addiction to sunset clouds
to dispense with this sickness of words
let wooded springs purify this old heart
azure clouds burnish the sun red

山水道之華于予成著述非天舌本窮借我筆端出寧
使煙霞痼且消文字疾林泉浣古心蒼靄浴紅日

泉香流石骨遠望以飛煙聽徹峰恆靜心通水得潺梅

花開十里茅屋祇三間馴虎長依座吟猿時護關山人

飄白髮竹杖過蒼巒晤笑疎鐘動迂迴古澗沿禪心清

欲絕不復信塵喧

perfumed springs ripple over skeletal outcrops
in the distance a hint of smoke, rising
I hear perpetual stillness in these hills
sense the rush of swirling waters
white plum blossoms blanket a dozen miles
save for this single, tiny hut
tigers, half-tame, loiter near my door
chattering monkeys guard my gate
a wild mountain-man, white hair streaming
tops the slate summit on a bamboo staff
caught unawares, I laugh at the distant bell
follow the twist and turn of an ancient stream

Zen-hearted, washed free of all desire
never again will I wander the noisy dust

mountain sounds carry a chill wisdom
an upwelling spring whispers subtle tales
pine breezes stir the fire beneath my tea
bamboo shadows soak deep into my robe

I grind my ink: clouds scraping across the crags
copy out a verse: birds settling on branches
as the world rolls right on by
its every turn tracing out non–action

山響發清慧泉聲語細微松風吹茗火竹陰透禪衣拭
硯雲開石臨書鳥下枝物情爲我轉轉處見無爲

老衲斑斕山影重草鞋無底印苔蹤歸家洗腳埋頭坐
冷煖從來只問心

my ragged cloak is streaked with mountain shadows
my torn-out sandals scrape bare prints through the moss
home again, I wash my legs, bury my head in my hands…
am I warm? am I cold? I no longer know

82

in the nearby mountains, a green mountain haze
on the distant sea, white sea clouds
the chatter of birds is soundless
the roar of gibbons—absolutely silent

前山山氣青後海海雲白鳥語本非喧猿啼眞是寂

秋山如錦畫雲物生餘輝倚杖看紅葉無聲共鳥飛

166

autumn mountains: brocades of light
the clouds: endless beauty
I lean on my staff, contemplate crimson leaves
silent: as the birds streaming above me

AFTER SHIH-TE

I climb these hills as if walking on air
body too light to fall
bamboo staff resting against a great stone
torn cloak snapping in the wind

a lone bird soars the azure depths
far distant springs reflected in its eye
carefree, singing a timeless song
gone—on a journey without end

登頂若天步身輕無險危
短筇同石立破衲逐雲飛孤
鳥入空翠眾泉生遠輝閑吟
不能已此路竟誰期

世情殊可哀山意不爲懼林木作衣裳詩文當狩獵心

閒如白雲身輕似紅葉猿鳥引吾前恣懷登且涉

157

how pitiful, the feelings of the world
still, the hills are not afraid
with forests of trees to clothe them
the hunting ground of poems and verse

my heart is free as the white clouds
body light as a crimson leaf
apes and birds pull me forward
lusty as ever, we rise up—cross over

when were the stones and trees born?
green, green, layer upon folded layer
granite hard, untouched by the snows
ancient, obstinate, unscathed by frost

the jade tree, just one old branch
but Scarlet Flowers will restore its color
glistening, glossy, endlessly radiant
or darkly sheltered: hidden in the world below

石樹生何代青青深幾倍堅貞雪不凋古勁霜難改玉
幹老一枝瓊花新五彩光澤照無窮蔭覆天下在

Notes

35. Personification is uncommon in Chinese poetry, but Shih-shu uses the technique fairly often. His mountain has flesh and bones, is lonely and aloof. We also see it undergo a transformation of coldness to warmth that is as much emotional as it is seasonal. Perhaps these two poles, cold and warm, also mark the two modes of the Tao—as unspeakable, unmanifest, and pre-cosmic and as an omnipresent life force scattered throughout each and every one of the "ten thousand things" that make up the world.

40. The price of reclusion in the beauty of nature is poverty and namelessness. Or, perhaps, this price is itself the reward.

134. Shih-shu could have followed the bustling coach across the plain into town and perhaps have encountered a sweet thing or two there. But he would prefer, it seems, to remain faithful to his own hills, his own pond. A light, but perfectly apparent, tincture of eroticism suffuses this poem.

92. Like Buddhist emptiness, the original Tao is without form or substance. Yet it is the source of all manifestations, all transmutations—"the mother of the ten thousand things," says Lao-tzu's *Tao-te ching*.

    The first two lines of the second verse are reminiscent of the opening passage of the recently discovered "lost Taoist text" the *Tao Yuan* (*Wellspring of the Tao*; translated in Robin B. Yates, *Five Lost Classics: Tao, Huang-Lao, and Yin-Yang in Han China*, Ballantine Books, 1997, p. 173), which as Yates points out is itself reminiscent of an early passage in the *Huai-nan Tzu*.

The five colors here are emblematic both of the Buddhist five senses and the Chinese five elements (earth, wood, fire, metal, and water). Their being swallowed up by one breath seems to bespeak the Tao's evolution outward to the ten thousand things and the subsequent return of the world (or of the Taoist mystic) back to this original formlessness. Outbreath. Then…inbreath.

133. The hermit's life has its difficulties. Being cold, lonely, and wet are among them. Flowers cast a mildly erotic glow here, although plum blossoms, the first flowers to emerge in spring, are perhaps not as promising as the lush peaches and lithe willows of poem

134. Way, of course, translates as Tao, the Way. This does not, however, make this a Taoist poem. The word "tao," in its metaphorical meaning of "spiritual path," was the common property of all Chinese religions.

149. This seems quite a dark poem. Technically the theme could be Buddhist impermanence, but perhaps it is really death that is at issue—the untimely end to an unfulfilled life (unless it is the dark mystery of the unmanifest Tao that marks our journey's end).

93. Old age, illness, and death are marks of Buddhist impermanence and sorrow. Having touched on death, Shih-shu here looks at old age. But, oddly, at the end of the poem it's hard once again to tell his exact meaning. Is this old couple pitiful in their infirmity, or blessed in their togetherness?

37. This is an odd meditation. First we are asked to cast aside both body and passions. But having seen the passage of autumn, we may yet, it seems, hope to know new springs still to come.

70. In the first stanza the poet conflates the goals of the Buddhist saints with those of the Taoist "immortals" (*hsien*).

137. This seems to be the account of a real dream. The Weaver Girl and the Herding Boy are two stellar constellations, as well as mythical lovers. Trapped on opposite sides of the Milky Way, they can meet only once a year, on the seventh night of the seventh month. Here the poet seems to become the object of the Weaver Girl's tryst. But just as things are getting nicely started, reality intrudes—and the poet wakes up. Chuang-tzu woke up thinking he might be a butterfly, but this is sadder still.

73. This is a very odd poem. It is just as scatalogical in Chinese as it is in English translation. Of course, Buddhist critiques of the sometimes pretentious Dharma are not entirely uncommon. The Ch'an master Tan-hsia, after all, chopped up an image of the Buddha for firewood. But to liken the Dharma to feces and urine? To reduce cosmology to defecation? Really! And it just gets worse. Are fur and hair meant as erotic images here? And who would laugh at the Black Wind of Death? Why does the poet end up peeing in the pond? Is there more here than meets the eye? Less? Just what is going on? Dear reader, it's up to you.

55. A number of Shih-shu's poems are based on the notions of Taoist alchemy. Among them, this expression of the unity of microcosm and macrocosm is fairly transparent, as is the sense that the true path will takes us back to the Tao. However, the final line is less clear. Is it perhaps an allusion to *Chuang-tzu*, chapter 20, in which Confucius praises swallows as the embodiment of fastidiousness?

94. The "man of no position" is a common Zen (Ch'an) pat phrase for the enlightened master. Tiger and dragon are yin and yang. Ox and horse are less clear, although the terms do

occur in Taoist alchemy as code names for two primary trigrams of the I-ching, *ch'ien* and *k'un*, as in the lines of a poem by the alchemical Taoist, Tzu-yang Tzu, the Master of Purple Yang: "Ox without horns / Horse without hooves / This horse, this ox / Father Ch'ien, Mother K'un." (As a two-character compound, *ch'ien-k'un* means "Heaven and Earth" or the universe.)

155. The first verse of this poem is not very clear, at least not to the translator. Although the idea that emptiness is a kind of narrative is rather attractive, the twin dragons and the azure dog are entirely puzzling. By contrast, the images of mountains in a bowl and astral entities in the human body are quite direct microcosm/macrocosm talk. The last line in the original Chinese contains a further amusing conceit. The characters translated as "snap" and "snarl" are *lao* and *hou*. Each of these consists of the "mouth radical" plus a second element. The radical marks them as onomatopoetic noise words, while the remainder of *lao* is the *lao* of Lao-tzu and the remainder of *hou* is the *k'ung* of K'ung-tzu (Confucius). Presumably this clues the close reader into the fact that Lao-tzu and Confucius were a couple of babbling windbags.

106. "Non-action": *wu-wei*

82. At times Shih-shu expresses doubts about the value of writing poetry—a common problem for Buddhist poets. Birds and gibbons offer, perhaps, a solution.

▪ After Shih-te (p. 165). Shih-shu presents himself as a Taoist immortal, about ready to abandon his staff and cloak, waiting to rise into the sky, eager to soar with the birds.

157. In this piece Shih-shu lets poetry, Buddhism, Taoism, and passion all get tangled up. This is his way to enlightenment, one supposes.

158. Stones and trees, of course, spell out Shih-shu's name. The jade tree is phallic, Scarlet Flowers ostensibly an alchemical elixir. Does Tao/Nirvana shine out from the world beyond? Or does it hunker down with us, here, in the world below?

CHING AN

Ching An *(1851–1912)*

Translations by J.P. Seaton

Introduction

CHING AN, A NATIVE of Hsing-t'an, in Hunan Province, entered the Fa-hua Monastery there at the age of seventeen. Orphaned early in life, he probably received most of his considerable secular education in the monastery, along with his religious training. Ching An was purportedly a gifted poet even as a child: it is said he was able to make poems even before he learned to write, chanting them to be transcribed. Although precocious literary ability is a common part of traditional literary hagiography, the extraordinary quality of his mature works makes this particular anecdote easy to believe.

Early in his career, he burned off two fingers as a votive offering to the Buddha, a spectacular gesture even within the tradition of self-mortification that accompanied much Buddhist practice in China. It earned him the by-name Pa-ch'ih T'ou-t'uo, The Eight-Fingered Monk. The episode also produced, much later in his life, one of the poems included in this selection, a disarmingly rueful look at youthful enthusiasm in which the mature poet asks, "Did I really think I could become a Buddha / one slice at a time?"

Ching An was the abbot of several famous monasteries, and his poetic reputation spread widely throughout both Ch'an and lay literary circles. His poetry certainly demonstrates the longevity of the Ch'an poetic tradition and its vitality during the difficult social and political climate of the late nineteenth and early twentieth centuries, when the Ch'ing dynasty was collapsing under the weight of its own corrupt senescence and the onslaught of Western colonialism. In the poems of this selection, the poet avoids both the

Buddhist technical vocabulary and overt moralizing that is a feature of Buddhist poetry by lesser poets of the tradition. He shows a deep familiarity with the lay poetic tradition; but, while allusions to the works of poets like the Ch'an layman Wang Wei of the T'ang are evident in many poems, his poems are always fresh, vivid, and original.

Wang K'ai-yun (1833–1916), a lay friend who was arguably the finest classical poet of the late Ch'ing, favorably compared Ching An's work to that of the legendary wild-man monk Han-shan. It is a surprising comparison, considering the fact that Ching An was a successful abbot and a recognized leader in the relations between the monastic community and the central government, but it is a particularly apt one. Like Han-shan's poems, Ching An's are sharply personal and even apparently iconoclastic. I have commented, at some length, on his poetic technique in a note to one of the poems in this selection.

Ching An was also compared by contemporaries to the famous late T'ang Buddhist poet Chia Tao (779–843), a selection of whose poems are translated in this book. One reason for the association of Ching An with Chia Tao may very well have been the practical role that he attempted to play in the world of politics. Unlike Chia Tao, Ching An didn't embrace Confucian orthodoxy and serve in the Imperial government. After the fall of the Ch'ing dynasty he did, however, go to Beijing to represent the many monks and great monasteries of Chekiang and Jiangsu Provinces. His attempt to help in the founding of a national Buddhist organization to protect the Buddhist cultural heritage and to promote a role for the sangha in the new Republic was unsuccessful. He died there, in residence at the ancient Fa-yuan Monastery, in 1912. Ching An was an extraordinary poet and a brilliant emblem of the vitality of the Ch'an tradition at the beginning of this century.

Note on Personal and Geographical Names

Though I have no doubt they were real people, I've been unable to locate either Shih-chia Tzu or the drunken calligrapher Hsu in either standard or specialized Buddhist biographical dictionaries. Neither have I been able to locate Lushan Temple in the standard geographical dictionary. The rest of the geographical names refer to places in the area in which Ching An lived most of his adult life—the scenic area in east-central China from Hangchou northward through Chekiang and Jiangsu—that was also the cultural center of China in the later dynasties. I hope that further research on the poetry and life of Ching An reveals him and his milieu in a clearer light, but, certainly, the poems reveal his art and his spirit in the clearest light possible.

ON THE ROAD: A SPRING DAY AT LING-FENG

Spring comes, together with a rush of feelings.
I go, alone, to knock at a grotto's gateway.

The grass by the stream rides green on my clogs:
The canyon clouds climb white on my robe.

Fallen flowers? With the stream's flow,
　　they'll get where they're going.
Wild birds? They'll fly along with me.

When I was near the end of the woodcutter's way
　　it was only the bell song led me out
from among the hillside's subtle iridescent blues and greens.

春日靈峰途中
春來多逸興獨去欵巖扉
落花隨水至野鳥伴人飛
澗草青承屐溪雲白上衣
樵路行將盡鐘聲出翠微

山銜雲飛窺人淨江挾濤聲入海長　　却羨巢松千歲鶴不知塵世有滄桑

迢遙鐘梵下斜陽寂寂巖花渡水香　　殿角一鈴風自語窗前萬木雨初涼

題麓山寺

In the shimmer of distance
the bell speaks pure Sanskrit
seeing off the slanting sun.

Secret, silent
blossoms beneath
the overhanging cliffs
send their fragrance on the stream.

In the single wind chime at the temple's eaves
the wind speaks for itself.

Before my window, ten thousand trees,
the rain's the first Fall chill.

The hills, locked in cloud essence,
pry into my purity.

The river carries the ancient sound of the billows
all the way to the sea.

I won't admire the thousand-year crane
that nests the ageless pine.

He doesn't know that in the human world
groves turn to seas.

ON THE SPOT WHERE SHIH-CHIA TZU
SITS IN MEDITATION

Ten thousand trees
cold forest
as I came up through the blue greens of the hillside

Wafting in the wind
white crane, my feathery head
a long time beyond scheming.

The sound of the stream
is, after all,
without a present, or a past.

The beauty of the mountain colors:
what could it have to do
with "right" or "wrong"?

The lush grass of the high pass
may certainly mislead
the wanderer's clogs.

Cliffside flowers
sometimes fall
on a robe that's sitting zazen.

If you ask the teacher
when
he came to sit on T'ien-t'ai Mountain:

"Green pines I planted
with my own hands:
ten hands' span, now."

題天臺十甲子老僧坐禪處

萬木森寒入翠微飄然鶴髮久忘機

澗草自迷遊客屐巖花時落坐禪衣

溪聲畢竟無今古山色何曾有是非

問歸何代天臺住手種青松已十圍

179

過徐酡仙故宅

野棠含雨梨花白不見高陽舊酒徒
門巷蕭條長綠蕪流鶯猶似勸提壺

PASSING BY WHERE HSU, "THE WINE-FLUSHED
IMMORTAL," USED TO LIVE

*("The Wine-flushed Immortal" was good at drinking and good at
doing calligraphy drunk. He called himself "the drunken wanderer
of Ssu-ming Mountain." For a longer discussion of this poem, see
the note at the end of this section.)*

Gate in a lane
chill, bleak, artemisia grows
and tall green weeds.

Mango birds, pretty girls
still come as if to urge you:
Drain the bowl!

Wild crab apple blossoms
mouth the rain.
Pear blossoms, white.

But no longer to be seen
high on the essence of the creative
that old wine bibber of Kao Yang.

DUSK OF AUTUMN:
WRITING WHAT MY HEART EMBRACES

I am the orphan cloud:
no trace left behind.

Come South three times now
to listen to the frosty bell.

When men see geese flying
they think of letters home.

Even the mountains grieve at the Fall:
they're wearing a sickly face.

But fine phrases are there too
to be plucked from the sad heart of Autumn,
and many an ancient poet ran into one on the road

I'm ashamed I've yet to realize
my monk's oath:

the fault's in this load of blue green hills I carry
many tens of thousands strong.

暮秋書懷

身作孤雲無定蹤南來三度聽霜鐘

人方見雁思鄉信山亦悲秋帶病容

佳句每從愁裏得故人多在客中逢

自嗟未了頭陀願辜負青山幾萬重

對雪書懷

四山寒雪裏半世苦吟中　鬢易根根斷詩難字字工

心肝徒自嘔言論有時窮　寂寂平生事蕭然傳夜鐘

FACING SNOW AND WRITING
WHAT MY HEART EMBRACES

At Mount Ssu-ming
in the cold in the snow
half a lifetime's bitter chanting.
Beard hairs are easy to pluck out
one by one:
a poem's words are hard
to put together.
Pure
vanity
to vent the heart and spleen;
words and theories, sometimes, aren't enough.
Loneliness, loneliness
my everyday affair.
The soughing winds
pass on the night bell sound.

TO SHOW YOU ALL,
ON THE FIRST MORNING OF THE YEAR

A thousand thousand worlds,
a single breath,
one turn of the Great Potter's Wheel.
The withered tree blossoms

in a Spring beyond illusion.
Pop!
The firecrackers bring me back:

the laugh's on me.
This year's man
is last year's man.

元旦示眾
大千一氣轉洪鈞枯木開花象外春
爆竹一聲翻自笑今年人是去年人

三遊雪竇

扶筇三上妙高臺又欲題詩掃石苔
野鶴閒雲應識我一年一度入山來

THIRD TIME WANDERING
TO CLOUD SLUICE PEAK

Propped on tough bamboo
three times now I've climbed
this tower of mysteries.

So I can write another poem
I brush the moss from stone.

The cranes in the clouds
must know me by now:

every year we both come here for the Autumn.

BEATING THE HEAT AT JADE LAKE

West of the painted bridge
east of the willow's shade:
ten *li* of flat lake:
water touching, holding, sky.
Not like it is among men,
bitter at the burning heat.
Monk's robe sits idle:
lotus blossoms: breeze.

碧湖消夏
畫橋西畔柳陰東十里平湖水接空
不似人問苦炎熱衲衣閒坐藕花風

夜坐

幽人夜不眠愛此碧虛月

涼風一颯然吹動梧桐葉

NIGHT SITTING

The hermit doesn't sleep at night:
in love with the blue of the vacant moon.
The cool of the breeze
that rustles the trees
rustles him too.

WRITTEN ON THE PAINTING "COLD RIVER SNOW"

Dropped a hook, east of Plankbridge.
Now snow weighs down his straw rain gear
    it's freezing.
The River's so cold the water's stopped running:
fish nibble the shadows of plum blossoms.

題寒江釣雪圖
垂釣板橋東雪壓蓑衣冷
江寒水不流魚嚼梅花影

歸雲

煙樹蒼茫疊翠微
道人長掩竹中扉
白雲也識山居味
不待鳴鐘已早歸

RETURNING CLOUDS

Misty trees hide in crinkled hills' blue green.
The man of the Way's stayed long
at this cottage in the bamboo grove.
White clouds too know the flavor
of this mountain life;
they haven't waited for the Vesper Bell
to come on home again.

OVER KING YU MOUNTAIN WITH A FRIEND

Sun sets, bell sounds, the mist.
Headwind on the road, the going hard.
Evening sun at Cold Mountain.
Horses tread men's shadows.

與長沙袁總戎過育王嶺
日暮煙鐘鳴歸路西風緊
夕陽在寒山馬蹄踏人影

題畫

一株兩株松三箇五箇竹
巖扉長寂寥祇有雲來宿

ON A PAINTING

A pine or two,
three or four bamboo,
cliffside cottage, long, solitary, silence.
Only floating clouds come to visit.

MOORED AT MAPLE BRIDGE

Frost white across the river
waters reaching toward the sky.
All I'd hoped for's lost
in Autumn's darkening.
I cannot sleep, a man
adrift, a thousand miles
alone, among the reed flowers:
but the moonlight fills the boat.

楓橋夜泊和唐人韻
白露橫江水接天秋懷黯黯不成眠
一身漂泊三千里獨宿蘆花月滿船

重過楊家橋
照水朱顏半已凋春風依舊柳千條
樓鴉數點斜陽裏不忍題詩過此橋

CROSSING THE YANG–CHIA
BRIDGE ONCE MORE

The face reflected in the stream's
lost half its youthful color.
Spring wind
is as it was before,
so too, the thousand willow boughs.
Crows perch to punctuate
the lines of slanting sunset.
It's hard to write
as I pass this place once more.

AT HU-K'OU, MOURNING
FOR KAO PO-TSU

Though he was young, Kao
was the crown of Su-chou and Hu-k'ou.
It was only to see if he was still here
that I came today to this place...
found a chaos of mountains
no word
this evening sun
this loneliness

湖口弔高伯足
高生才調冠三吳爲問人間尚有無
今日卻過湖口縣亂山無語夕陽孤

寒巖枯木一頭陀
結習無如文字何
自笑強書塵世字
卻嗔倉頡誤人多

自笑
其一

自笑

LAUGHING AT MYSELF I

Cold cliff
dead tree
this knobby pated me...
thinks there's nothing better than a poem.
I mock myself, writing
in the dust, and
damn the man who penned the first word
and steered so many astray.

LAUGHING AT MYSELF II

Slices of flesh made burnt offering
　　　to the Buddha.
Just so, I came to know myself
a ball of mud dissolving in the water.
I had ten fingers. Now, just eight remain.
Did I really think I could become a Buddha
　　　one slice at a time?

其二
割肉燃燈供佛勞
了知身是水中泡
祇今十指惟餘入
似學天龍吃兩刀

Note to "Passing by Where Hsu, 'The Wine-flushed Immortal,' Used to Live"

I often set aside the draft of a poem I love in the original when it becomes apparent that it will require a footnote in English. This poem is so nice and so representative of a number of features of Ching An's style that I have paraphrased in the translation in an attempt to maintain the poem's integrity in American English. I am providing this note to help the reader understand the techniques that the paraphrase tries to capture. The first paraphrase is in line two, where the mango birds (or orioles, if you prefer) are a conventional metaphor for fashionable prostitutes, or professional "entertainers." The play of sensuality in Ching An's work is intentional and appropriate to a worldly Zen that acknowledges that while phenomena are empty they are nonetheless attractive. The drunken calligrapher was certainly visited by fashionable ladies of the entertainment quarter, and what he did with them was their business. So, for the reader who needs to be reminded to look at birds and flowers in a Chinese poem as "the birds and the bees," I have added "pretty girls" at the denotational level, even though they are only there as an allusion, or at the connotational level, in the original.

The second paraphrase comes in the last line. There I have trampled on my own rules for translation by inserting an interpretive line before the literal rendering. The verbatim translation of this line is "Not / See / High / Yang / Old / Wine / Disciple." In this "literal" rendering of the line I have read High Yang as a geographical name, something perfectly justifiable, and certainly what Ching An intended us to do at the first level of interpretation. Following Western convention, I have thus rendered it as "Kao Yang," giving only the transliteration of the character for *high* or *tall* (*Kao*) and for *Yang* (the *Yang* of *Yin and Yang*). This is typical of the way translators render Chinese geographical names into English: for example, the name of the T'ang dynasty's imperial capital, Ch'ang-an, is usually transliterated rather than translated as *Long* (or *Eternal*) *Peace*.

There are places in T'ang poetry, particularly after the An Lu-shan rebellion turned the capital into a perpetual center of armed struggle, where poets like Tu Fu clearly used its names with a certain ironic relish, but it is generally acceptable to simply transliterate its name. Here, though, a look at the meaning of the two characters involved may make it clear why I've been tempted to break my own rules of translation and even to write a footnote. *Kao* means "high," "tall," or, in more formal discourse, "eminent." *Yang* means "Yang," as in Yin and Yang; it is the active principle, the essence, the virtue of creativity. Old Mr. Hsu, drunk as a High Lord and full of Yang, attracts pretty entertainers, and creates characters in wild grass writing. He's the image, or perhaps the envy, of the spirits. And, lest all this wild Yang threaten the puritanical, let it be noted that Ching An clearly points out that the old drunk is gone, dead. However, I doubt Ching An's point was intended to be puritanical: some Ming and Ch'ing Zen men were often as wild as some modern Tibetan Buddhists.

To take it even a step further, I'll point out that the wine bibber in the last line is derived from the *Shih Chi* (*Records of the Grand Historian*) of Ssu-ma Ch'ien, the first great historian of China. It is quite possible that Ching An derived this allusion indirectly from a quotation of the *Shih Chi* in a poem by Kao Shih, the seventh-century scholar-official-poet and friend of Tu Fu. Ching An, despite his humble social origins, was a truly erudite man. Though he may very well have grabbed the allusion from the enormous poet's phrase book, *P'ei-wen Yun-fu*, as was the common practice of Ch'ing and even Ch'ing Zen poets, it is a good grab. The presence in this poem of other vocabulary from the Kao Shih poem suggests that Ching An wanted his readers to know that source and probably to read it.

The allusion suggests another layer of meaning in the poem too (the only good reason for an allusion). Li I-chi, the historical man behind the allusion, is presented in the original source (*Shih Chi*, 97) as a man who lived a life of reclusion during the last chaotic years of the Ch'in dynasty, becoming known in his own neighborhood as a "madman." When Li I-chi was later identified as a Confucian scholar in hiding by the first Emperor of the Han (ca. 200 B.C.E.), he had to claim he was merely a "drunk" so that the emperor would grant him an audience, at which he offered his services to him. Before he was tutored by the likes of Li I-chi, the self-proclaimed "wine bibber of Kao Yang," the first Emperor of the Han used to express his opinion of Confucianism by urinating in the ceremonial hats of "Confucians" when they came for an audience.

As the Ch'ing dynasty began to collapse under the domination of the alien Manchus, many of the Chinese literati excused themselves from service to its emperors on any grounds conceivable. Many became recluses, feigning exotic personalities, simply to avoid being called to service. The allusion may thus be an attempt to provide an explanation, or an excuse, for the calligrapher's drinking habits that is simultaneously a restatement of Ching An's well-known anti-Manchu political stance. Or it may simply be Ching An's way of investing the late Mr. Hsu with an aura of respectability by suggesting that he's not just a drunk. The one might be an example of what I've heard called politically engaged Buddhism. The other might represent compassion for the old calligrapher's survivors.

This poem is real live Zen, it seems to me. The sound of one damned good poet getting really deep into the complexities of the simple life.

Epilogue

NINE FLOWER MOUNTAIN

Perched on the edge of
A cloud-torn ridge
High in the mountains
Of Chiuhuashan
A shaved-head nun
Sweeps alone the entrance
To her vine-covered cave

A few tufts of
Wind-blown bamboo
The persistent pine
Growing straight out of stone

A place so graceful
So tough and real
Even the Immortals
Feel a shiver up the spine

She spots us ascending
The narrow path
Sets aside the broom
Pours water for tea

Afterward
We burn a stick of incense
Leave a twenty
On the smoky
Lamp-lit altar

Then follow her
Up a rain-polished trail
To Moon Viewing Peak
Where the whole of China
Is spread at our feet

I watch her point out waterfalls
That drape like silk
From old granite cliffs
And wonder what brought her here
So many years ago

A poorly arranged marriage
Some magnificent
Loss of face
Or the simple pleasure
Of living alone
In the profound silence
Of mountains

In the afternoon
Black clouds swirl
Slowly up the valley floor
A signal
We must make our way back
To buses
And dust
And a billion scattered souls

But before we leave
Our nun gives us
Gingered plums
And a walk through
The garden

Where we left her
Grinning
At tiger tracks in the sand

Finn Wilcox
  Mount Chiuhuashan
  September 1991

Index of First Lines

About the Contributors

PAUL HANSEN is a painter, poet, and translator of Chinese poetry who lives on Fidalgo Island in northwest Washington. He is the author of *Rimes of a Riverrat* and has translated four collections of Chinese poetry: *Before Ten-Thousand Peaks* (Copper Canyon, 1980); *The Nine Monks* (Brooding Heron, 1988); *Lin He-Jing: Recluse Poet of Orphan Mountain* (Brooding Heron, 1988); and most recently *Lin He-Jing's Art of Poetry* (Woodworks Press, 1997). His translations have also recently appeared in *A Drifting Boat: An Anthology of Chinese Zen Poetry* and *The Columbia Anthology of Traditional Chinese Literature*.

MIKE O'CONNOR, a native of the Olympic Peninsula, Washington State, is a poet and translator. After many years subsistence farming in the Dungeness River Valley and cedar logging and tree planting in the Olympic Mountains, he traveled to Taiwan, the Republic of China, to begin more than a decade of Chinese studies and work as a journalist. He recently returned to the U.S. and resides with his wife, Liu Ling-hui, a choreographer and dance teacher, in Port Townsend, Washington. He holds an M.F.A. degree in writing and poetics from the Naropa Institute, a Buddhist college in Boulder, Colorado.

His principal books of poetry include *The Basin: Life in a Chinese Province* and *The Rainshadow*. His primary works of translation include *Setting Out*, a novel by Taiwan's Tung Nien; *The Tienanmen Square Poems*; two selected works of the T'ang poet Chia Tao; and *Only A Friend Can Know*—a mix of original poems and translations on the Chinese theme of *chih-yin*—published in *Mudlark*, an electronic journal of poetry and poetics [www.unf.edu/mudlark].

RED PINE (Bill Porter) was born in Los Angeles in 1943 and grew up in Northern Idaho. Following a tour of duty in the U.S. Army, he attended college at U.C. Santa Barbara and graduate school at Columbia University. Uninspired by the prospect of an academic career, he dropped out of Columbia halfway through a Ph.D. program in anthropology in 1972 and moved to a Buddhist monastery in Taiwan. After four years with the monks and nuns, he finally struck out on his own and eventually found employment at English-language radio stations in Taiwan and Hong Kong, where he interviewed local dignitaries and produced more than a thousand programs about his travels in China. His published translations include the complete poems of Cold Mountain (Han-shan), Pickup (Shih-te), and Big Shield (Feng-kan), as well as the works of Stonehouse (Shih-wu), Sung Po-jen (for which he was awarded a PEN West translation prize), and Lao-tzu (for which he was a finalist for the same award). He is also the author of *Road to Heaven: Encounters with Chinese Hermits*. He currently lives in Port Townsend, Washington.

JAMES SANFORD was born in Gunnison, Colorado, on a bitterly cold day early in 1938. Most of his childhood was spent in Denver, after which he ended up in California as a callow undergraduate with a beard. In 1960 he graduated from U.C. Berkeley with a degree in linguistics. The following years he enlisted in the army, learned some Chinese, got married, spent sixteen months in Taiwan, entered graduate school, had two children, and spent a year in Japan. In 1972 he received a Ph.D. from Harvard University's program in Asian Languages and Cultures. Since 1971 he has taught Asian religions in the Department of Religious Studies at the University of North Carolina at Chapel Hill. Most of his publications have been in the areas of Japanese Zen, Shingon esotericism, and Buddhist poetry. He lives twelve miles out in the country in a ramshackle house with a large deck, in the company of a fine wife and fifteen or twenty mostly personable, though occasionally pushy, animals.

ANDREW SCHELLING (b. 1953) is a poet and wilderness activist. He grew up in "Thoreau country," where early influences were New England's resurgent conifer forests, jagged granite, and Boston's Asian art collections. After nearly two decades in Northern California—Sanskrit language studies, ethnology and natural history, companionship with urban poets of the Bay Area—he moved to Boulder, Colorado in 1990 on the Front Range of the Southern Rockies, where he teaches poetry, Sanskrit, and wilderness writing at The Naropa Institute. Recent books include *Old Growth: Poems and Notebooks 1986–1994* (Rodent Press), *The Road to Ocosingo* (Smoke-Proof), and *The Cane Groves of Narmada River: Erotic Poems of Old India* (City Lights). Schelling has received translation awards from The Academy of American Poets and the Witter Bynner Foundation for Poetry.

J.P. SEATON was born in West Lafayette, Indiana, where he grew up in a house that was less than a block from the woods and only a mile walk from the Wabash River. It's still a mile from the river, but it's three miles from the woods these days. The house he lives in today is in the woods, just half a mile up Chicken Bridge Road from the Haw River, about ten miles through the loblolly pines from Pittsboro, N.C., a little town where it will still be possible, for a few years, to live a half block from the woods.

Educated at Indiana University (Ph.D. 1968), he currently teaches Chinese language and literature at the University of North Carolina at Chapel Hill. His work has been published in magazines and anthologies, and he is the author of several books, including *I Don't Bow to Buddhas: Selected Poems of Yuan Mei* from Copper Canyon Press. Most recently, he collaborated in the translation of the *Tao Te Ching* by Ursula K. LeGuin and co-authored with Sam Hamill a version of *Chuang Tzu*.

BURTON WATSON is among the most revered translators of classical Chinese and Japanese poetry. Born in 1925 in New Rochelle, NY, he served three years in the navy during World War II before beginning Chinese Studies at Columbia College. Among his dozens of translations of major works of Japanese and Chinese history, poetry, and philosophy, his *Chuang Tzu* is an acknowledged classic. He has edited *The Columbia Book of Chinese Poetry*, translated the *Lotus Sutra*, and received both the Gold Medal Award of the Translation Center at Columbia University and the PEN Translation Prize. Formerly Professor of Chinese at Columbia University, he now lives in Niigata, Japan and devotes full time to translation.

What to Read Next
from Wisdom Publications

When I Find You Again, It Will Be In Mountains
The Selected Poems of Chia Tao
Translated by Mike O'Connor

"A gorgeous tapestry."—Anne Waldman, Naropa University

Where the World Does Not Follow
Buddhist China in Picture and Poem
Translated and introduced by Mike O'Connor
Photography by Steven Johnson

"A beautiful marriage of word and image."—*Publishers Weekly*

Zen Master Poems
Dick Allen

"In the tradition of Mary Oliver and David Whyte, Dick Allen's *Zen Master Poems* offers spiritual insights in lucid, seemingly effortless verse."—*Tricycle*

Daughters of Emptiness
Poems of Chinese Buddhist Nuns
Beata Grant

"A landmark collection of exquisite poems scrupulously gathered and translated."—*Buddhadharma*

About Wisdom Publications

Wisdom Publications is the leading publisher of classic and contemporary Buddhist books and practical works on mindfulness. To learn more about us or to explore our other books, please visit our website at wisdompubs.org or contact us at the address below.

Wisdom Publications
199 Elm Street
Somerville, MA 02144 USA

We are a 501(c)(3) organization, and donations in support of our mission are tax deductible.

Wisdom Publications is affiliated with the Foundation for the Preservation of the Mahayana Tradition (FPMT).